Student Guide to the World of the Bible

Contents

What is the Bible?	2	Daily Life	17
Writing	3	Palestine in Jesus' Time	18
Old Testament Time Chart	4	Jesus in Galilee	19
Fathers of the Nation	5	Parables of Jesus	20
Freedom: Moses and the Exodus	6	Miracles of Jesus	21
The Promised Land	7	The Synagogue	22
God's Anointed: Saul, David & Solomon	8	Herod's Temple	23
The Divided Kingdom	9	Jerusalem: Jesus' last days	24
The Tent of God's Presence	10	Jesus' Resurrection Appearances	25
Gods' House: King Solomon's Temple	11	The Good News Travels	26
The Farmer's Year	12	Travel in Bible Times	27
The Jewish Festivals	13	Paul's Missionary Journeys	28
Kings and Prophets	14	People of the New Testament	30
People of the Old Testament	15	The Seven Churches of Asia Minor	31
Clothing	16	Index	32

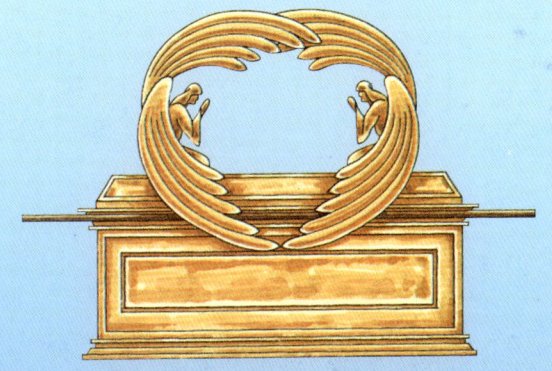

What is the Bible?

The Bible is made up of a "library" of 66 books, 39 in the Old Testament, 27 in the New. The writings of the **OLD TESTAMENT** first appeared as separate scrolls in Hebrew; we do not know how or when they were first gathered into a single volume. The 39 books of the Old Testament vary in authorship and style and can be divided into four major groupings:

Law
Sometimes called the Pentateuch, or "five scrolls."

History
Tracing the story of God's people from their entry into the Promised Land to the Exile.

Poetry and Wisdom
Full of proverbs, riddles, parables, warnings and wise sayings.

Prophecy
God's prophets explained what had happened in the past; spoke out against evil in the present; and told of what God would do in the future.

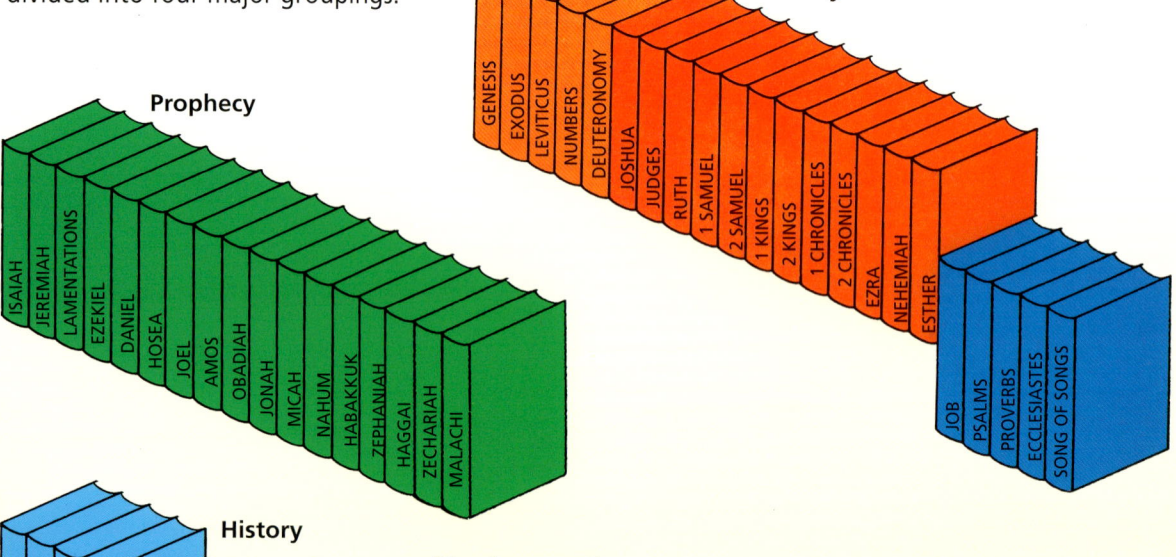

The Apocrypha
The Apocrypha is a collection of books and additions to the Old Testament books written between 300 BC and AD 100. They were not accepted by the Jews as part of the Old Testament Scripture, and most Protestant denominations do not accept them as part of genuine Scripture.

The Books are interesting and valuable historical documents that range from historical narratives to pious fiction.

The 27 books of the **NEW TESTAMENT** were written in Greek and can also be divided into different types of writing:

History
The book of Acts and the four Gospels. The Gospels, however, are not simply historical records; they were written to persuade readers to believe in Jesus, and form portraits of Jesus as the Messiah.

Letters
These include Paul's letters to churches in various cities, his letters to individual Christians, and letters written by other apostles.

Revelation
This book opens with letters to seven churches in Asia Minor, but continues with disturbing visions about the Last Days.

Writing

People did not write on paper in Bible times, but on clay tablets, pieces of pot, waxed boards and even bits of wood. People also started writing on parchment, made from sheep-skin, and on papyrus, a type of paper made from papyrus reed, which grows near the river Nile.

People used different tools to write on the different surfaces. To write on wax or on wood, they used a sharp-pointed stylus; to write on papyrus or parchment, they used a reed brush or quill pen.

In Old Testament times, pages of writing were often joined together by their edges and rolled up, to make a scroll. But by New Testament times, people had begun sewing pages together at their edges to make hinged books like ours.

Language

The Old Testament was originally written in Hebrew. Hebrew has 22 consonants in its alphabet, but no vowels. The characters of the alphabet are different from ours, and Hebrew is read from right to left instead of left to right.

Some parts of the Bible were written in Aramaic, which was closely related to Hebrew. Most ordinary people in Palestine spoke Aramaic in Jesus' time.

The New Testament was first written in the Greek of ordinary people, which is called Koine Greek. The Greek alphabet had 24 letters, which look different from the letters in our alphabet.

Above: In Bible times, official records, histories and inscriptions were often made on stone tablets such as this.

Above: People often wrote short messages in ink or with a sharp point on pieces of broken pottery, called *ostraca*.

Above: A wooden stylus was used to scribe marks onto clay writing tablets.

Right: A simple waxed writing tablet such as school children used in New Testament times.

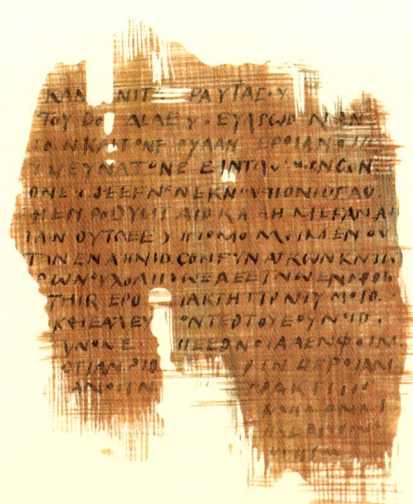

Above: This papyrus document contains verses from the book of Acts.

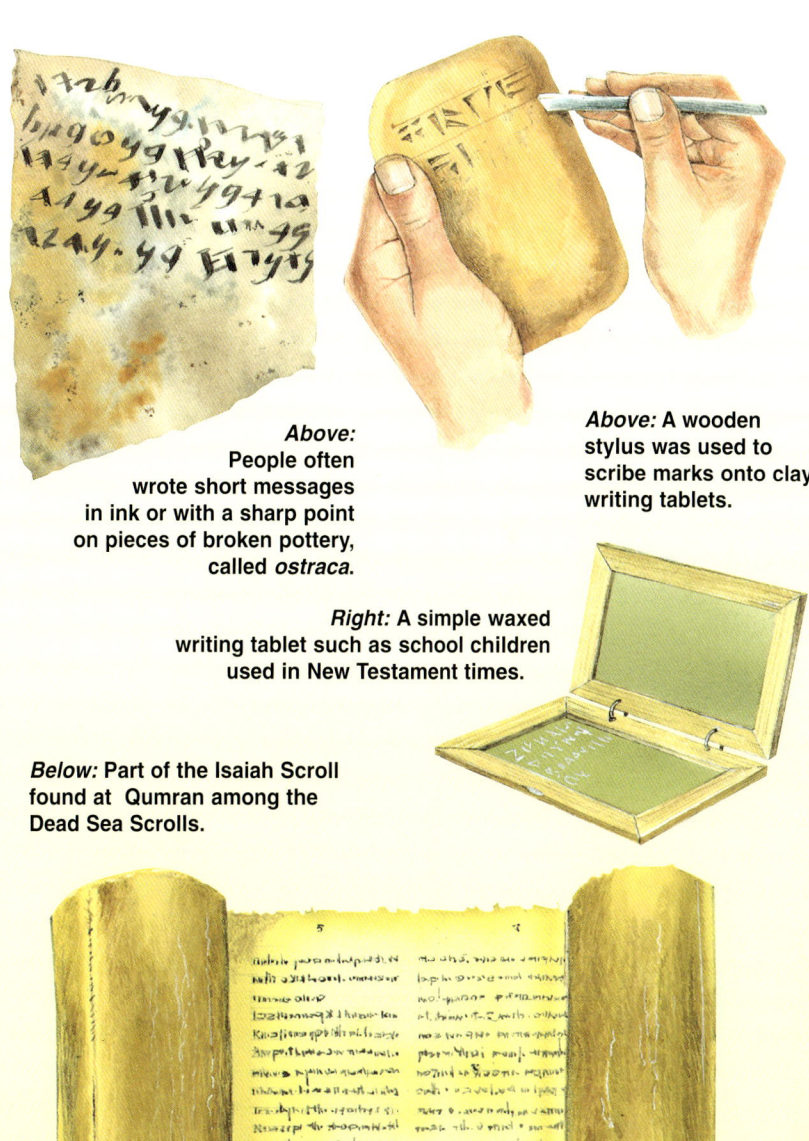

Below: Part of the Isaiah Scroll found at Qumran among the Dead Sea Scrolls.

Old Testament
TIME CHART

Abraham
Abraham set out from Mesopotamia on his great journey to the Promised Land.
God promised that through him all people would be blessed (Genesis 12:1–25:11). He was given a son, Isaac, in his old age (Genesis 21:1-7, 24:1–28:9).

Jacob
Isaac's son Jacob was forced by famine to go down to Egypt; his people settled there, and, years later, were forced into slavery (Genesis 25:19–35:29, 43:1–50:14).

Moses
Moses led the Hebrew people, Abraham's descendants, out of Egypt (Exodus 1:1–12:51). In the wilderness they were given the Ten Commandments. Eventually, after the death of Moses, the Israelites entered the Promised Land and occupied it (Joshua 1:1–12:24).

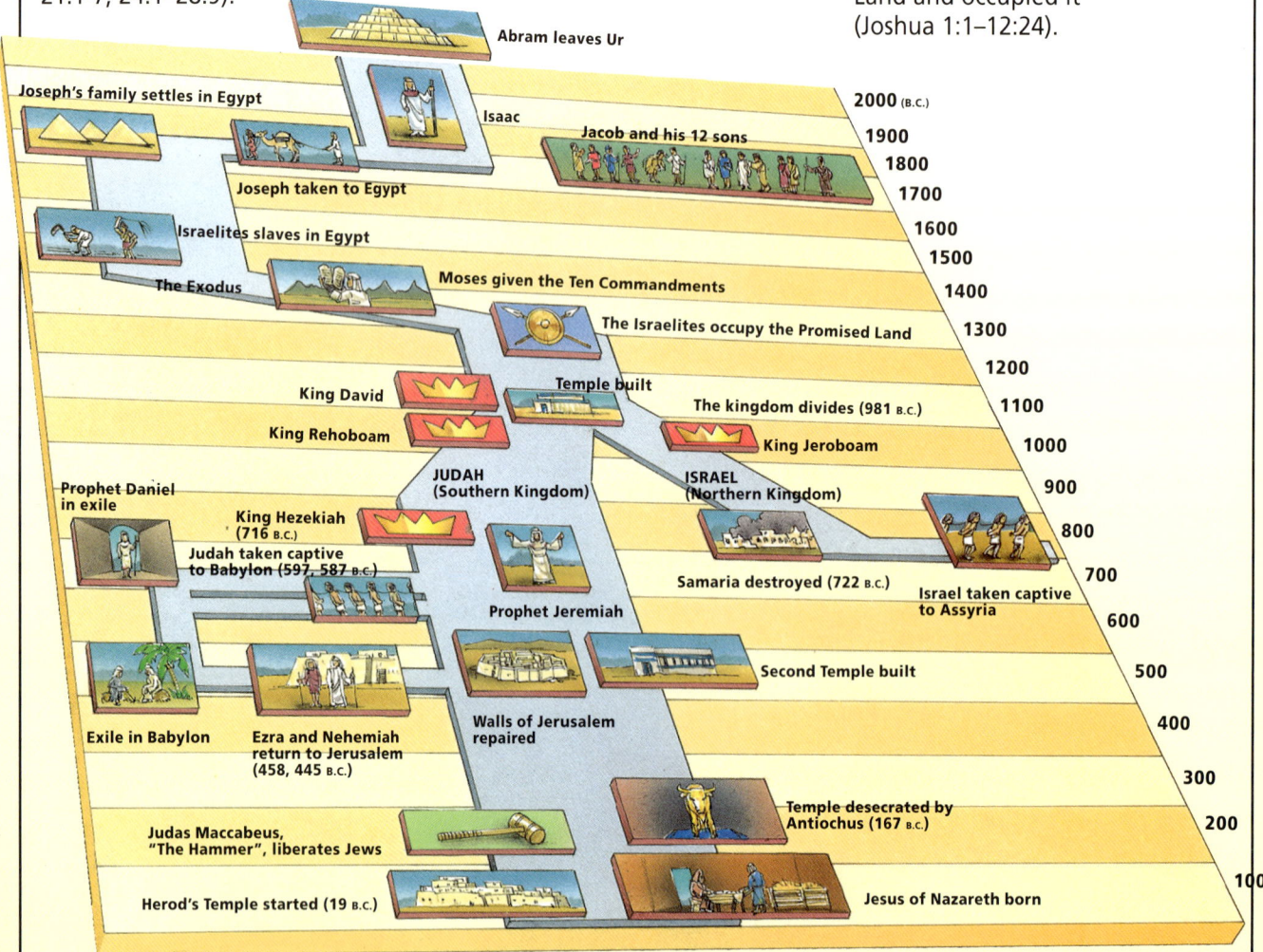

Judges and kings
As the nation of Israel developed, they were led first by judges (Judges 2:16–16:31, 1 Samuel 1:1–8:22) and then by a succession of kings (1 Samuel 9:1–31:13; 2 Samuel 1:1–24:23; 1 Kings 1:1–11:43). After the death of Solomon, the kingdom divided into Israel and Judah (1 Kings 12:1–22:53; 2 Kings 1:1–25:30).

Captivity
When the Assyrian Empire rose to power, Israel was threatened with invasion. Despite God's warnings to his people through the prophets, the northern kingdom (Israel) was taken into captivity by Assyria in 722 BC, and the southern kingdom (Judah) by Babylon in 587 BC (2 Kings 17:1-23, 25:1-30).

Return
The Jews only returned from exile in Babylon to Palestine by stages, to set about reclaiming their land and rebuilding Jerusalem and the Temple (Ezra 1:1–6:22; Nehemiah 1:1–7:73a). Many of the Jews did not make this journey back to Palestine.

Fathers of the Nation

Abraham

God wanted to create a people who would have a special relationship with him, so that all other nations would be able to see how their trust in God brought them wholeness. God called Abraham, promising that his descendants would become a great nation. Through them, all people would see God's purposes and love. Abraham left Ur, on the river Euphrates, and eventually came to Canaan (Genesis 12:1-9), the Promised Land, and to Egypt (Genesis 12:10-20). He brought with him his wife, Sarah, and his nephew, Lot. Abraham's wife was a fine example of faith and prayerfulness.

Above: Abraham had large flocks of sheep and herds of cattle.

Isaac

Abraham had a son, Ishmael, by his servant Hagar. But in old age, Sarah, Abraham's wife, gave birth to a long-awaited son, Isaac, so enabling the fulfilment of God's promise to make a great nation of Abraham's descendants (Genesis 18:1-15, 21:1-7).

Jacob

Isaac married Rebekah, and had twin sons, Esau and Jacob. Jacob, the younger son, won the inheritance by deceiving his father (Genesis 27:1-40). He fled to Mesopotamia to escape his brother's vengeance, and there married his uncle Laban's daughters, Leah and Rachel (Genesis 27:41–28:5, 29:15-30).

Jacob had twelve sons; his favourite, Joseph, was sold as a slave by his jealous brothers. After being wrongfully imprisoned in Egypt, Joseph rose to become chief minister of Pharaoh, bringing the rest of his family to Egypt when famine came (Genesis 37:1-36, 39:1–47:31).

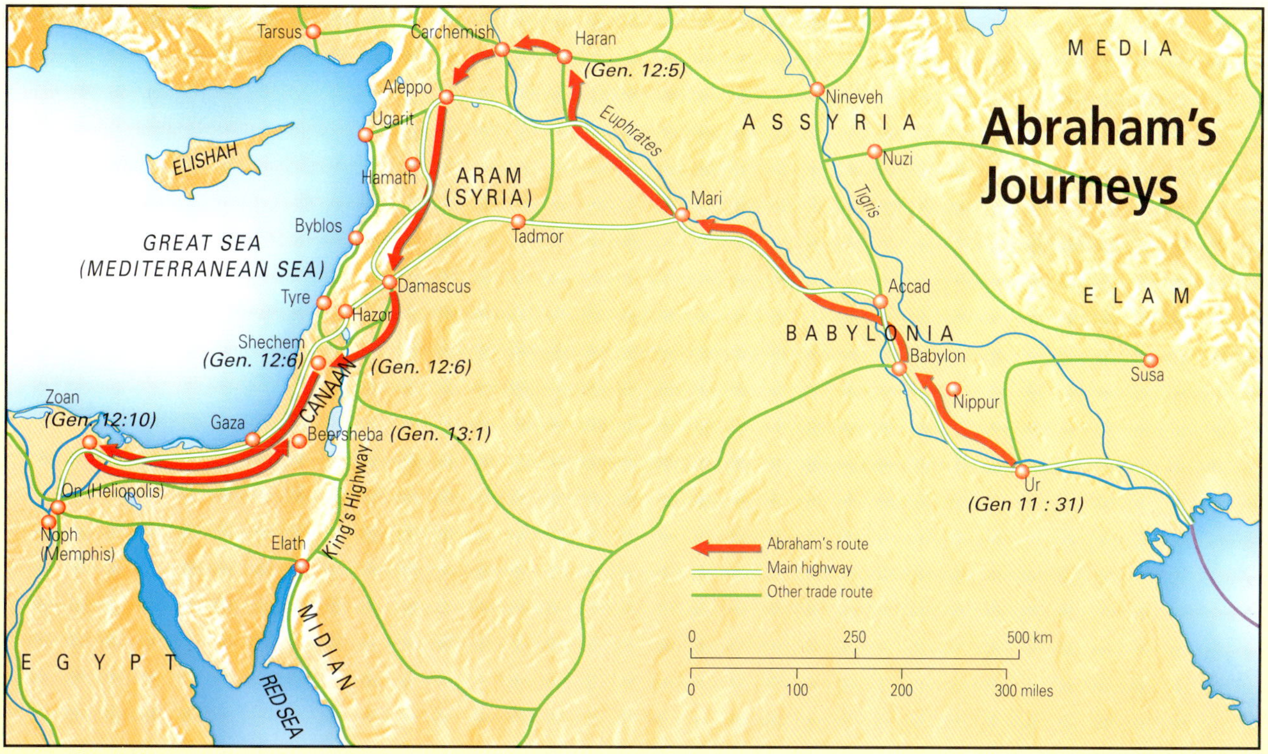

Freedom
MOSES AND THE EXODUS

The Exodus
The Israelites, or Hebrews, remained in Egypt for four generations. In time they were no longer welcomed as visitors, but were pressed into slave labour (Exodus 1:1-22).

They did not understand God's purpose for them, and failed to carry out his mission. Therefore God sent Moses to set his people free, revealing himself to Moses as I AM (Exodus 3:14). It was only after Egypt had been struck with a series of terrible disasters that the Hebrews were able to leave (Exodus 7:14–12:42).

The Ten Commandments
God now began to teach his people how he wanted them to be his special people. The message of Exodus is not only about freedom from oppression, but also about God's providing for his people's needs as he led them through the wilderness (Exodus 15:22–17:16).

At Mount Sinai God renewed the covenant he made with Abraham, binding himself to all the Israelites. The Hebrews were also given a special code to live by, a code which included the Ten Commandments and many other rules and instructions (Exodus 19:1–24:18). God showed his people that they were to worship him alone, and to live in a way pleasing to him.

Wandering in the desert
The Israelites spent 40 years in the wilderness, until the death of Moses. While they were wandering in the wilderness, the Israelites sent spies into Canaan. Most of the spies returned with dismaying reports, though the land was rich and fertile (Numbers 13:1-33).

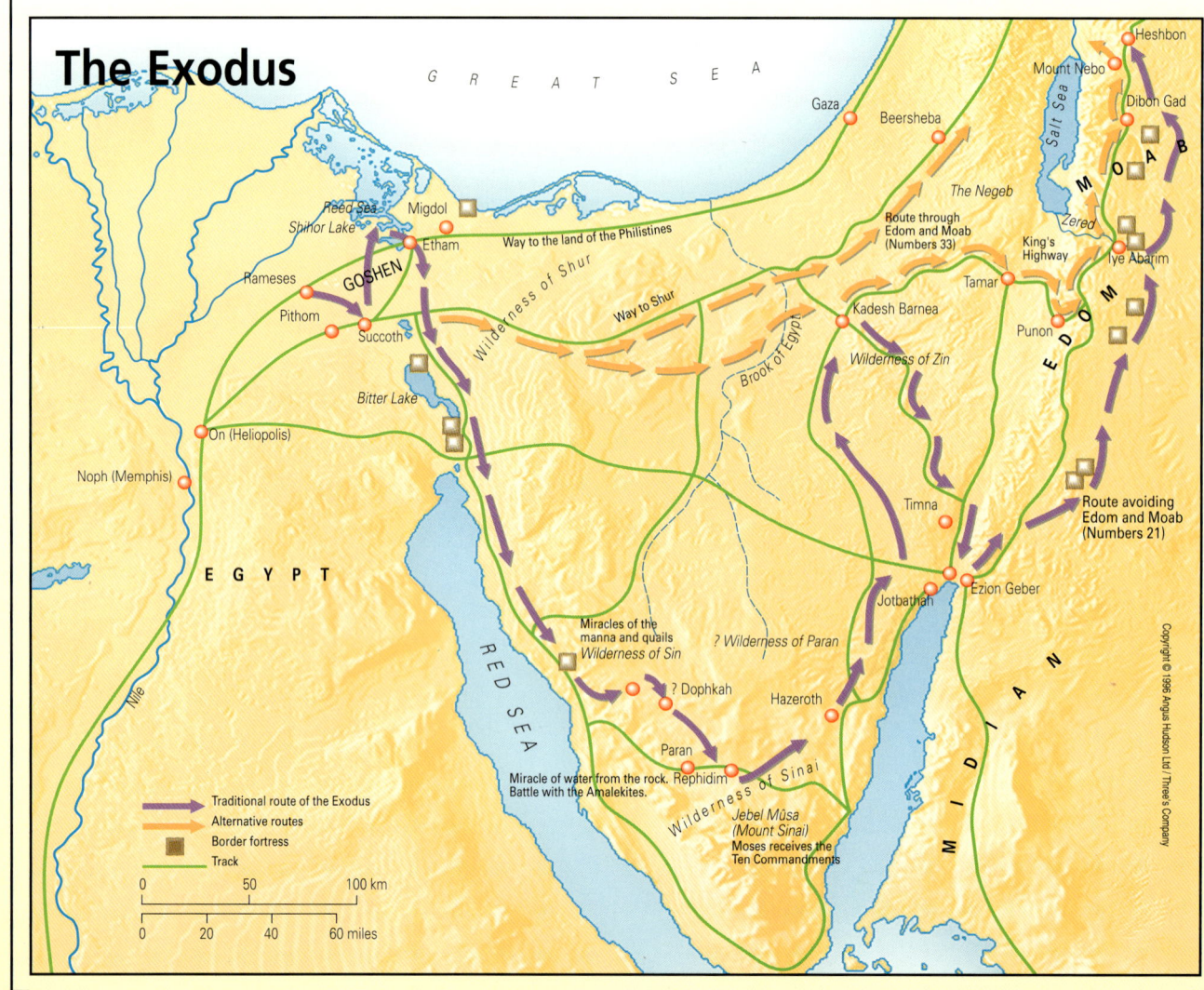

The Promised Land

Not until Moses had died, and Joshua took over as leader, did the Israelites finally enter the Promised Land. According to the book of Joshua, they now had to conquer the land and settle it among the different tribes. The book of Joshua records three campaigns: a central thrust through Jericho and Ai, a southern campaign and a northern campaign (Joshua 5:13–8:29, 10:1–11:23).

Although the Israelites won many victories, the Philistines still controlled the coastal cities, and the Canaanites many inland towns. After they entered the Promised Land, the Israelites faced the choice of serving God or the Canaanite gods.

The Israelites set up six cities of refuge, which served as places of asylum for people who had committed uninentional manslaughter (Numbers 35:6-25.

High place and well at Dan, northern Israel.

Areas settled by the 12 tribes of Israel

God's Anointed
SAUL, DAVID & SOLOMON

King Saul
Although God had given his people a land of their own, they turned their backs on God, and tried to become like the surrounding nations. The Israelites thought that if, instead of relying on God's rule, they had a king they could see, they would conquer their enemies. King Saul was anointed by Samuel to be the first king of Israel. But he openly disobeyed God, and died at the battle of Gilboa (1 Samuel 9:1–31:13).

King David
Samuel also anointed David, Jesse's youngest son. God promised that a descendant of David would be a king who reigned forever. David failed many times, but always loved God and returned to him (1 Samuel 16:1–30:31; 2 Samuel 1:1–24:25).

King Solomon
Under David's son, Solomon, the kingdom prospered. Solomon became renowned for his wisdom, and during his reign the great Temple was finally built in Jerusalem. Yet Solomon, too, turned away from God, and built temples to foreign gods (1 Kings 1:1–11:43).

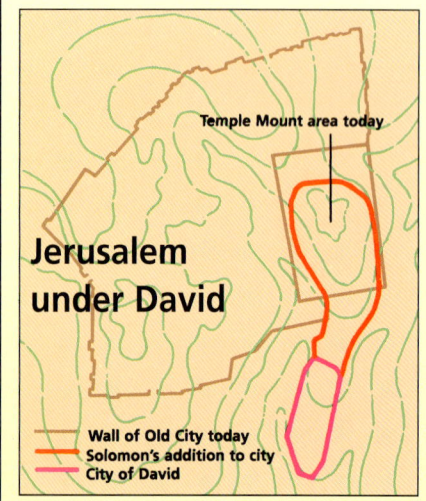

Jerusalem under David
- Wall of Old City today
- Solomon's addition to city
- City of David

The Divided Kingdom

Israel

After Solomon's death, the ten northern tribes rebelled and set up a separate kingdom of Israel, ruled by Jeroboam, with its capital at Shechem and worship centres at Dan and Bethel (1 Kings 12:1-23). Omri, a ninth-century king of Israel, founded a new capital called Samaria (1 Kings 16:24). Omri was succeeded by such kings as Ahab and Jehu (1 Kings 15:25–22:40, 22:51-53; 2 Kings 1-8:15, 9:1–13:25, 14:23-29, 15:8-31, 17:1-6).

Judah

David's successors continued to rule the southern kingdom of Judah from the capital, Jerusalem (1 Kings 14:21-31, 15:1-24, 22:41-50; 2 Kings 8:16-29, 11:1–12:21, 14:1-22; 15:1-7, 15:32–16:20, 18:1–25:30). This division continued until the Exile.

Babylonian warrior.

Israelite archer.

The Tent
OF GOD'S PRESENCE

While they were wandering in the desert, the Israelites built the Tabernacle, a special tent where they worshipped God. Each time they halted, they erected the Tabernacle in the middle of the camp, to show that God was at the centre of the nation's life.

The tent
The Tabernacle had a framework of acacia wood, covered by four layers of material, decorated linen curtains inside, and waterproof skins outside (Exodus 26:1-37).

Inside the tent
Inside the tent were two rooms. The small, inner room was the Holiest Place, entered only by the high priest, only once a year. Here stood the Ark of the Covenant, containing the tablets of the Ten Commandments, a pot of manna and Aaron's rod (Exodus 25:10-22; Hebrews 9:4).

The Holy Place
In the Holy Place, the outer room, stood the altar of incense, a seven-branched candlestick, and the table of showbread (Exodus 25:23-40, 30:1-10).

The sacred enclosure
The Tabernacle itself was surrounded by a curtained enclosure which could be entered only by priests and Levites. In front of the Tabernacle stood the bronze laver, where the priests ritually washed themselves, and the altar, where animals were sacrificed (Exodus 27:1-21).

Left: An artist's impression of the Ark of the Covenant.

Below: An artist's impression of the Tabernacle.

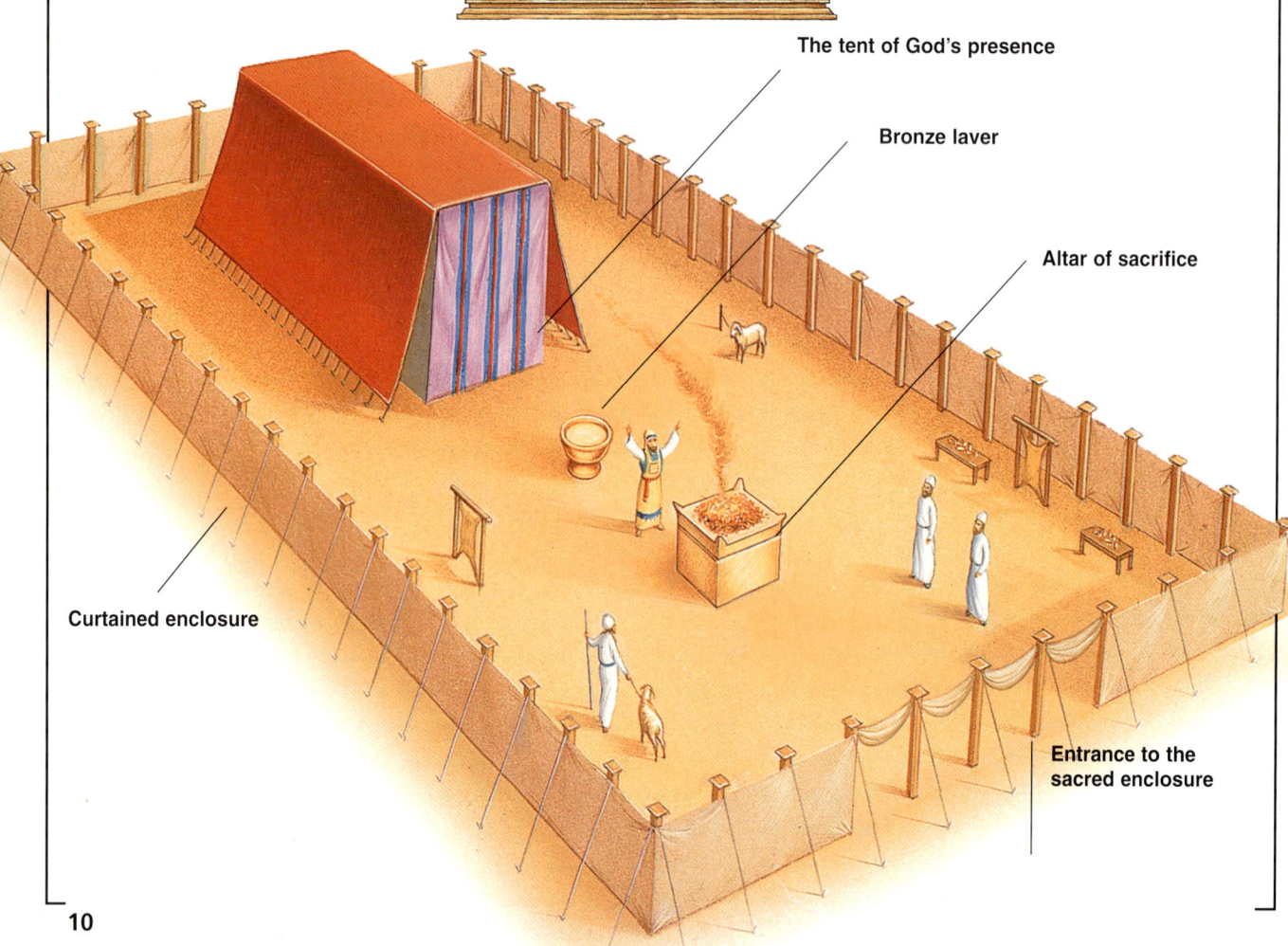

The tent of God's presence
Bronze laver
Altar of sacrifice
Curtained enclosure
Entrance to the sacred enclosure

God's House
KING SOLOMON'S TEMPLE

Following the conquest of Canaan, the Israelites stopped carrying the Tabernacle wherever they went. Finally, when the monarchy was established, King David brought the Ark of the Covenant to Jerusalem, planning to build a temple there (2 Samuel 6:1-19). But it was his son Solomon who actually built the first Temple.

Like the Tabernacle
Built of stone, the Temple was similar in its ground-plan to the Tabernacle, but much larger. It was panelled inside with cedarwood imported from Lebanon. Like the Tabernacle, the Temple housed the altar of incense, the table of showbread, lampstands and, in the Holiest Place, the Ark of the Covenant (1 Kings 5:1–6:38, 7:13–8:11).

Not a church
The Temple was not a meeting-place for God's people, like a modern church; only priests were permitted inside it to perform the ritual sacrifices and other duties. Solomon's Temple was destroyed when the Babylonians captured Jerusalem in 587 BC (2 Chronicles 36:15-19).

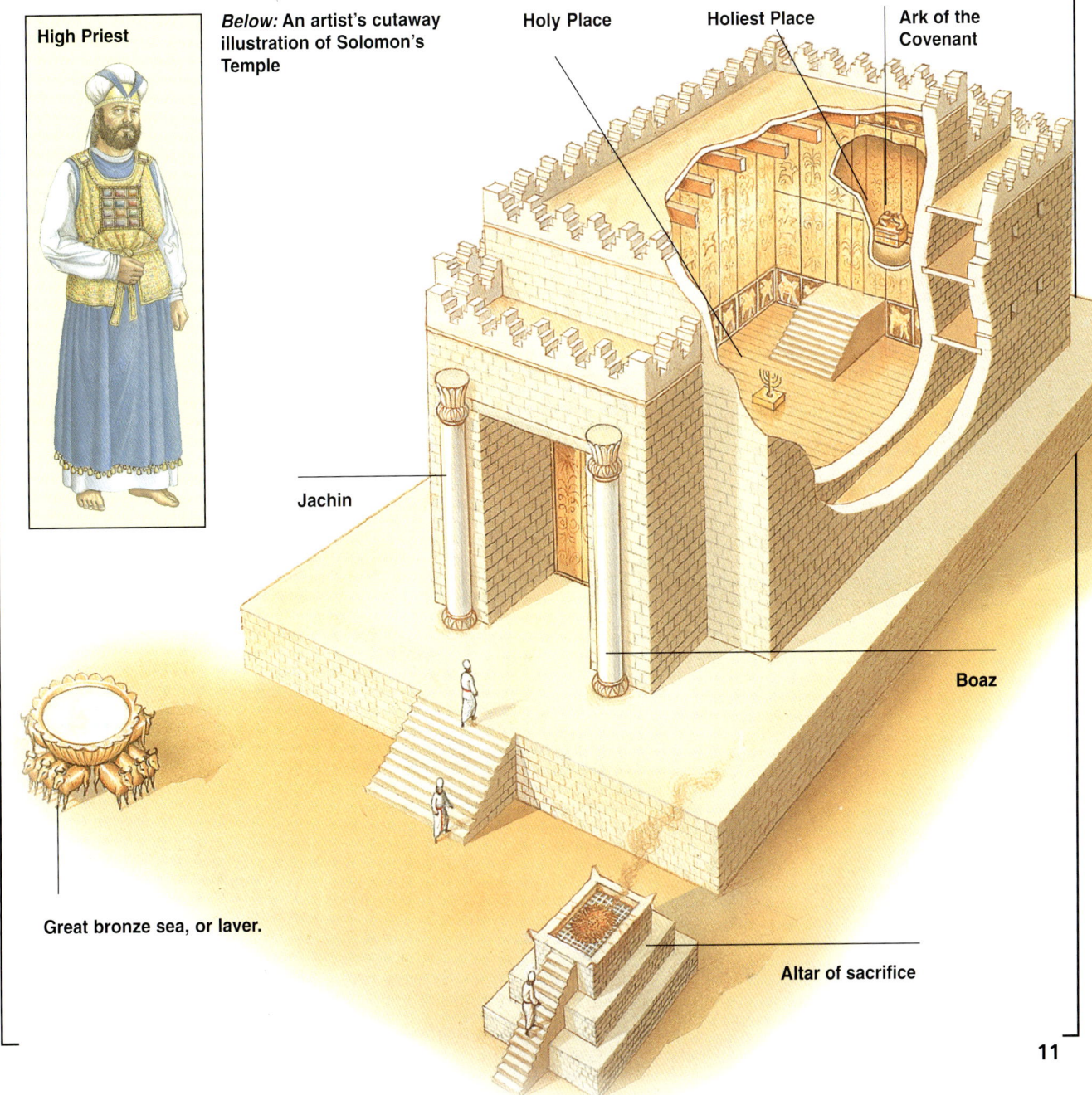

Below: An artist's cutaway illustration of Solomon's Temple

- High Priest
- Holy Place
- Holiest Place
- Ark of the Covenant
- Jachin
- Boaz
- Great bronze sea, or laver.
- Altar of sacrifice

The Farmer's Year

In Bible times, most people had some involvement with farming, every family having at least a small plot of land.

Grain
The main crops were wheat and barley. Following the autumn rains, the farmer ploughed the soil, and sowed the grain by hand. If there were winter rains, he could harvest the crop in April or May.

Harvest
The farmer would cut the grain with a sickle, leaving the sheaves in the field to dry. Next he threshed the grain on a threshing-floor, where oxen trod the grain from the ears of corn. After this, the farmer winnowed the grain, throwing it in the air to separate the grain from the lighter chaff, which blew away. Finally, the grain was sieved and stored away in sacks or large jars.

Fruit
The Israelites also grew fruit such as grapes, figs and olives as well as melons, dates, pomegranates and nuts. They also often cultivated vegetables such as beans, lentils, onions and cucumbers, and some herbs.

Animals
Sheep and goats were herded both for their meat and their milk, and for their wool and hair, which could be utilised for making garments. Farmers would often use asses for load-bearing, and oxen for pulling the plough.

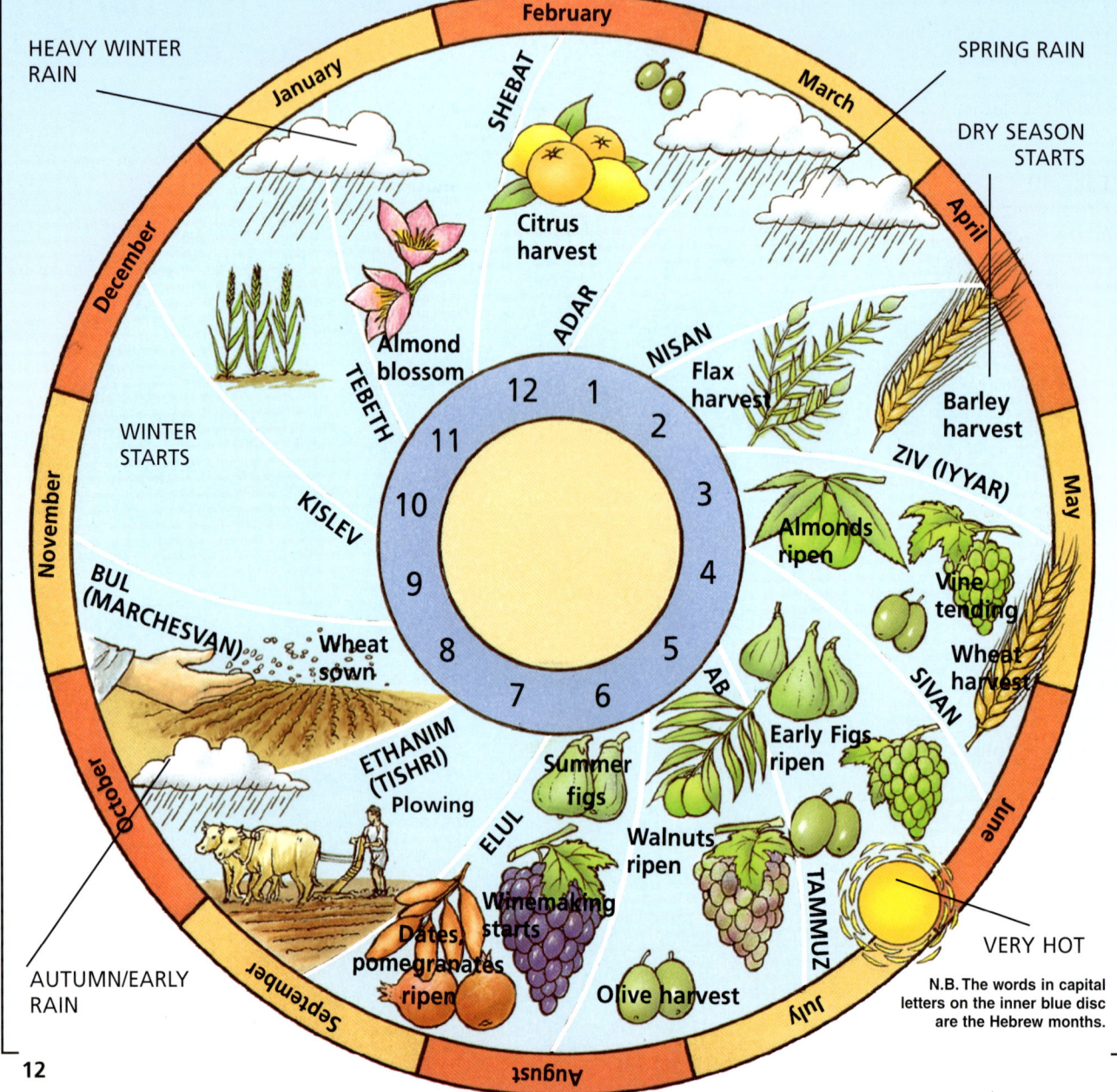

N.B. The words in capital letters on the inner blue disc are the Hebrew months.

The Jewish Festivals

God gave the Jewish people numerous feast days, or festivals, to celebrate different events through the year. Many of the feasts were originally farming festivals. The **Feast of Passover**, the **Feast of Weeks** and the **Feast of Tabernacles** were the three major festivals.

Feast of Passover (*Pesach*) celebrated Israel's deliverance from slavery in Egypt. On 14 Nisan each Jewish family ate their own Passover meal (*Seder*), re-enacting the first Passover (Exodus 12:1-49).

Feast of Unleavened Bread was the seven days following Passover, when Jewish families ate unleavened bread (Bread of Affliction), to remember the 40 years wandering in the wilderness (Leviticus 23:5-8).

Feast of Weeks (**Harvest**, or **Pentecost**) started seven full weeks (50 days) after cutting the first sheaf (*Omer*) and was to give thanks for God's blessing on the harvest (Leviticus 23:15-22).

Feast of Trumpets (*Rosh Hashanah* – **New Year's Day**) (Leviticus 23:23-25), recalled God's creation of the world and was celebrated on 1 Tishri.

Day of Atonement (*Yom Kippur*) was the most solemn holy day, of national confession, on 10 Tishri, when the high priest went into the Holiest Place of the Temple to sprinkle blood of the sacrifice (Leviticus 23:26-32).

Feast of Tabernacles (*Sukkoth*, **Booths**, or **Ingathering**), a week's celebration of the harvest, 15-21 Tishri, when the Jews lived in temporary shelters of branches (booths) to remember God's care for the Hebrews during their journey from Egypt to Canaan (Leviticus 23:33-43).

Feast of Lights (*Chanukkah*) was the Feast of Dedication, on 25 Kislev, to celebrate Judas Maccabeus' victory and the rededication of the Temple in 165/4 BC. Known as the Feast of Lights because an eight-branched candlestick is used, with an extra light to light the others on each of the eight days of the feast, recalling the miraculous provision of oil at the first celebration (2 Maccabees 10:1-8; John 10:22).

Purim is celebrated during 13-15 Adar and marks the deliverance of the Jews through Esther (Esther 9:1-32).

New Moon
The Jews celebrated the beginning of each month (Numbers 28:11).

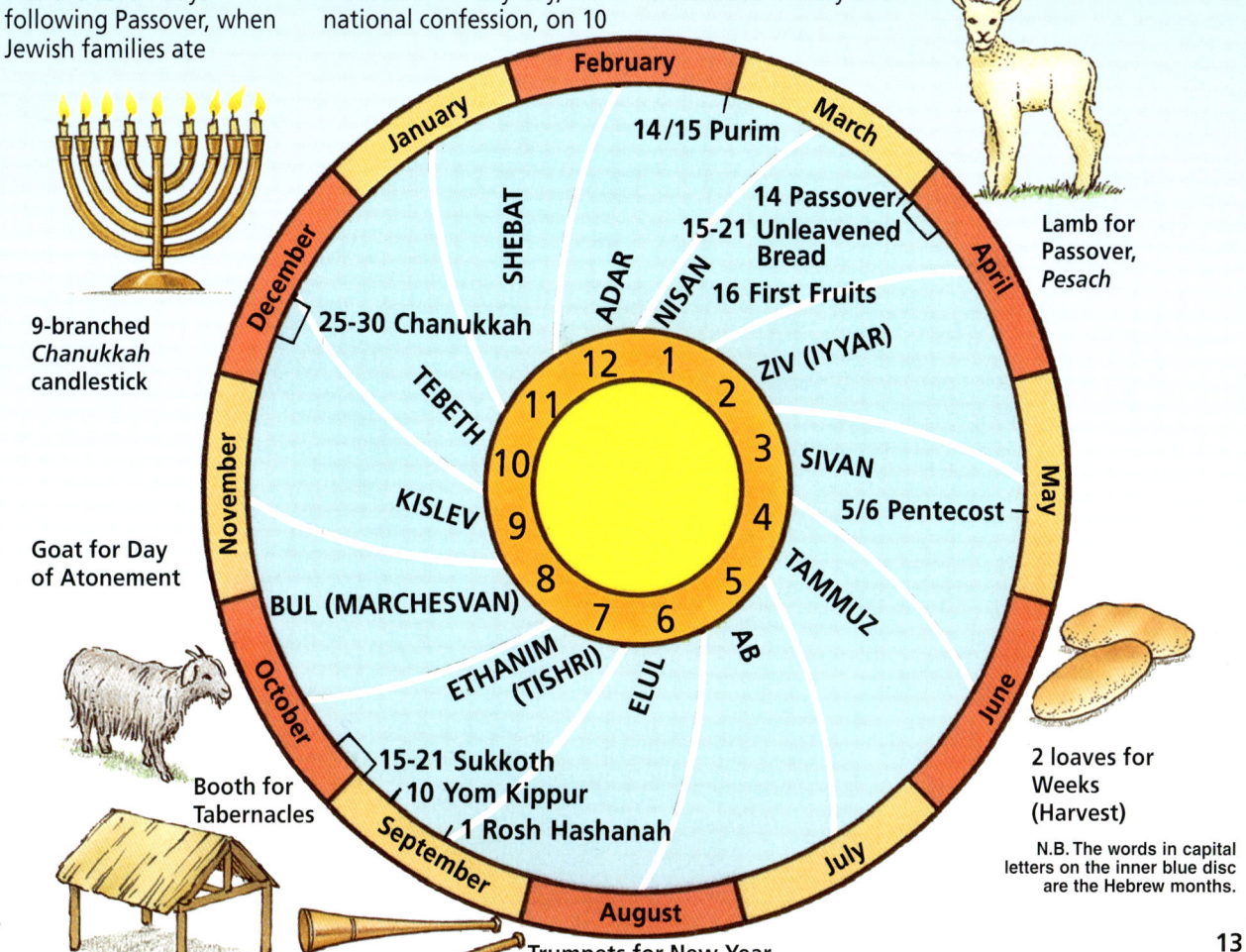

9-branched *Chanukkah* candlestick

Goat for Day of Atonement

Booth for Tabernacles

Trumpets for New Year, *Rosh Hashanah*

Lamb for Passover, *Pesach*

2 loaves for Weeks (Harvest)

N.B. The words in capital letters on the inner blue disc are the Hebrew months.

Kings and Prophets

Two kingdoms now emerged, Israel in the north and Judah in the south. Both became powerful and wealthy during the reigns of Jeroboam II and Uzziah, but the prophets Amos and Hosea condemned their corruption and materialism.

With the accession of Tiglath-pileser III (745-727 BC), Assyria became a major threat. King Hoshea of Israel turned to Egypt for military aid, prompting an attack from the new Assyrian king, Shalmaneser V, in 724 BC Hoshea was arrested and Samaria was besieged for three years

An artist's impression of the Assyrian siege of Lachish.

before finally collapsing (2 Kings 17:5-6). Its inhabitants were deported to Assyria.

King Hezekiah of Judah provoked the new Assyrian king, Sennacherib, who sacked 46 cities in Judah, including the Lachish, and then marched on Jerusalem. However, before he could capture the city, his army was ravaged (2 Kings 20:35) and he withdrew.

Egypt encouraged Jehoiakim, king of Judah, to rebel against Babylon in 600 BC, provoking a further Babylonian invasion in 598. Jehoiachin succeeded to the throne of Judah and surrendered Jerusalem to Babylon in 597. He and many Judeans were deported to Babylon, while a puppet king, Zedekiah, replaced him (2 Kings 24:18). Judah was persuaded to rebel yet again, and Jerusalem was finally burned in 586, and its inhabitants taken into exile (2 Kings 25:1-12).

This time-chart shows the years of ministry of the prophets and the reigns of the kings of Judah and Israel (1 Kings 12:1-22:53; 2 Kings).

	Judah		**Israel**	
Prophets	**Kings**		**Kings**	**Prophets**
Shemaiah	• Rehoboam 931-913		• Jeroboam I 931-910	Ahijah
	• Abijam 913-911			
	• Asa 911-870		• Nadab 910-909	Iddo
			• Baasha 909-886	
			• Elah 886-885	
Azariah			• Zimri 885-884	
Hanani			• *Tibni 885-880	
			• Omri 885-874	
	• Jehoshaphat 870-848		• Ahab 874-853	Jehu
			• Ahaziah 853-852	Elijah
Jahaziel	• Jehoram 848-841		• Jehoram 852-841	Elisha
	• Ahaziah 841		• Jehu 841-814	
Joel	• Athaliah 841-835			
	• Joash 835-796		• Jehoahaz 814-798	
			• Joash 798-782	
	• Amaziah 796-767		• Jeroboam II 782-753	
	• Uzziah 767-740		• Zechariah 753-752	
Isaiah			• Shallum 752	
Micah			• Menahem 752-742	
	• Jotham 740-732		• Pekahiah 742-740	
			• Pekah 740-732	Amos
	• Ahaz 732-716		• Hoshea 732-722	Hosea
	• Hezekiah 715-687			
	• Manasseh 687-642		*Fall of Samaria 722*	
	• Amon 642-40		*Israel in captivity– no kings*	
Zephaniah	• Josiah 640-609			
Huldah	• Jehoahaz 609			
Habakkuk	• Jehoiakim 609-598			
Jeremiah	• Jehoiachin 598- 597			
Ezekiel	• Zedekiah 597-587			
	Fall of Jerusalem 587		*See 1 Kings 16:21–22	

People of the OLD TESTAMENT

Aaron
Aaron, Moses' brother, became the first high priest of Israel. He founded the priesthood of Israel, but gave way to the people's demand in the wilderness for an idol, allowing the making of the golden calf.
Exodus 4:10-16, 17:10-12, 32:1-35

Abram (Abraham)
The founder of the Jewish nation, Abraham left Ur to travel to the land God had promised to him and his descendants. His barren wife, Sarah, gave birth to a son, Isaac, who enabled God's promise to be fulfilled that Abraham would become father of a great nation.
Genesis 11:26–25:10

Adam
The first man, Adam, created by God to be like him, was placed in the Garden of Eden. When he disobeyed God's command, by eating fruit from the forbidden tree, the whole creation was affected, and death entered the world.
Genesis 2:4–3:24

Daniel
A high-born Jew, Daniel was taken as a captive to Babylon, and trained as an adviser at King Nebuchadnezzar's court. God gave him wisdom, enabling him to interpret the king's dreams. When rivals plotted his downfall, and he was thrown into a lions' den, God saved him.
Daniel

David
Youngest of Jesse's sons, David was working as a shepherd when Samuel anointed him king, to replace Saul. David slew the Philistine champion, Goliath, but aroused Saul's jealousy, as a result of which he had to flee into hiding. After the death of Saul, David was crowned king. He made Jerusalem his capital, and brought the Ark of the Covenant there. David was a great king, a poet who wrote many of the psalms.
1 Samuel 16:1–1 Kings 2:11

Deborah
Deborah, the only woman judge, was one of the most successful judges of Israel. Her commander, Barak, defeated the Philistines, allowing 40 years free of foreign domination.
Judges 4:1–5:31

Elijah
The prophet lived in the time of the wicked King Ahab, and was sent to tell Ahab that God was sending a drought. Later, he defeated the prophets of Baal in a contest on Mount Carmel, and denounced Ahab for the murder of Naboth. Elijah trained Elisha to take over from him.
1 Kings 17:1–2 Kings 2:12

Elisha
Elisha took over from Elijah as prophet of Israel. He worked many miracles, including the healing of the Syrian army commander Naaman's leprosy.
1 Kings 19:16-21, 2 Kings 2:1–8:15, 9:1-37

Esther
Esther, who became queen of Persia, kept secret that she was Jewish. The king's chief minister planned to wipe out all the Jews, but Esther managed to save her people, by pleading with the king. Her victory is remembered every year in the Jewish festival of Purim.
Esther

Eve
Adam's companion, Eve, was the first woman. When she ate fruit from the forbidden tree, death entered the world, and Adam and Eve were ejected from Eden.
Genesis 2:18–3:24

Ezekiel
A Jewish prophet who was taken as a prisoner to Babylon, where he continued prophesying.
Ezekiel

Ezra
A Jewish priest and teacher of the Law who led some of the Jews back from exile in Babylon. He worked with Nehemiah to restore the Law.
Ezra 7:1–10:17; Nehemiah 8:1-18

Gideon
A judge of Israel who defeated the Midianites by guile.
Judges 6:1–8:32

Hezekiah
Judah's twelfth king; Hezekiah restored and re-opened the Temple and introduced religious reforms.
2 Kings 18:1–20:21; 2 Chronicles 29:1–32:33

Isaac
Isaac was born to Abraham and Sarah when his parents were very old. Later, Abraham was tested by God and told to sacrifice his son, but at the last minute an angel stopped him. Isaac married Rebekah and had twin sons, Esau and Jacob.
Genesis 21:1–28:5

Isaiah
Isaiah was a great prophet who lived through the reigns of Uzziah, Jotham, Ahaz and Hezekiah. During his time, the nation was threatened by Assyria; Isaiah foretold that, though his people would be taken into exile, they would eventually return. He also prophesied the coming Messiah.
2 Kings l9:1–20:19; Isaiah

Jacob
Jacob, Isaac's son, deceived his father into giving him the eldest son's blessing, and also bought his brother Esau's birthright. Jacob married Leah, and, later, her sister Rachel, and had twelve sons. After Jacob wrestled with a stranger, God gave him the name 'Israel'.
Genesis 25:21–35:29, 37:1-35, 42:1–49:14

Jeremiah
A prophet who ministered during the reigns of the last five kings of Judah, Jeremiah was unpopular because of his message of doom for the nation.
Jeremiah; 2 Chronicles 35:25, 36:21-22

Jonah
A Hebrew prophet whom God sent to denounce the citizens of Nineveh, Jonah was the first prophet to a heathen nation. He fled to sea; God saved him from drowning by means of a great fish.
Jonah

Joseph
Joseph, Jacob's favourite son, was sold into slavery in Egypt as a result of his brothers' jealousy. Thrown into prison on false charges, he later rose to prominence after correctly interpreting Pharaoh's dreams. When famine came, Joseph invited his family to Egypt, to escape its effects.
Genesis 37:2–50:26

Joshua
Moses' successor, Joshua led the Israelites into Canaan, conquered it and divided it between the twelve tribes.
Exodus 17:8-14, 24:13; Numbers 14:6-9; Deuteronomy 31:7-8,14,23, 34:9; Joshua

Miriam
As a child, Miriam helped her brother, Moses, escape death. Later she became a prophetess; at one time she opposed Moses' leadership, and was punished with leprosy.
Exodus 2:4-8, 15:20-21; Numbers 12:1-15, 20:1

Moses
Moses, the leader who freed his people, the Hebrews, from slavery in Egypt, was brought up by the king's daughter. Called by God to set his people free, Moses led his people out of Egypt and across the Red Sea. On Mount Sinai, God gave him the Ten Commandments. Moses died in Moab before the Israelites entered the Promised Land.
Exodus 2:1–Deuteronomy 34:12

Rebekah
Rebekah married Isaac, and suggested to her son Jacob that he trick his father into giving him the blessing.
Genesis 24:1–28:5

Ruth
Ruth left her home country, Moab, to return to her mother-in-law's home in Bethlehem, where she married Boaz, great-grandfather of David.
Ruth

Samuel
Samuel, the last of Israel's judges, was also one of the first prophets. At the end of his life he anointed Saul as Israel's first king. When Saul disobeyed God, Samuel anointed David to be king after him.
1 Samuel 1:1–4:1, 7:2–13:15, 15:1–16:13, 19:18-24, 25:1

Sarah
Abraham's wife, Sarah became the mother of Isaac in her old age, in fulfilment of God's promise.
Genesis 11:29–23:20

Solomon
Solomon, perhaps Israel's most famous king, was David's son by Bathsheba. Under his rule, the nation prospered, and his wisdom became a by-word. He built the first Temple in Jerusalem, but his marriages to foreign wives led to his turning away from God to false gods.
2 Samuel 12:24; 1 Kings 1:1–11:43; 1 Chronicles 22:5–23:1; Proverbs 1:1, 10:1, 25:1

Clothing

Most people living in Bible times wore simple clothing. The basic male garment was a loin-cloth. Over this, most men wore an inner and an outer garment. The inner garment was normally of linen or wool, and had long sleeves. It was fastened with a belt, and fell to the knees or ankles.

The outer garment, worn on top of this, was normally a square cloak made of animal-skin or wool. It was worn draped over one or both shoulders. A man was regarded as naked without it. He could also use it at night to sleep in. Wealthy men often wore beautifully embroidered outer garments of fine linen.

Women's clothing

Women, too, wore a simple under-garment, though it was usually higher at the neck, and often reached right down to the ankles. Women's clothes were usually white in colour, though some women wore black or blue. Rich women, like their men-folk, wore fine linen, dyed purple and red, and decorated with jewels, gold, silver and elaborate embroidery. Women also wore simple head-coverings rather like modern prayer shawls.

Below: **A pair of leather sandals from Bible times.**

Daily Life

Ordinary peoples' homes were very simple and usually built of mud, or lath and plaster. Although houses sometimes consisted of only one or two rooms, in villages small houses were often built with four rooms around a central courtyard, where the animals could shelter. In the cities the houses were built close together, but were sometimes two storeys high. Houses had flat roofs, often only 6 feet (1.8 meters) from the floor. On the roof, constructed from brushwood, earth and clay, the family could rest, sleep and work.

Inside the house

Doors were low and framed by wooden or stone doorposts; they rotated inwards and could be barred from within. Windows were small, unglazed and sited high in the wall, with additional light provided by small oil-lamps. Peasants possessed little furniture, apart from coarse skins which were unrolled at night on the raised platform made of beaten mud where the family slept.

Housework

The woman of the house did housework – cooking, cleaning, spinning, weaving and sewing. She would also help sometimes in the fields and vineyards, and teach her children in their early years.

There were normally just two meals each day: a breakfast of bread, fruit and cheese; and a larger supper of meat, vegetables and wine. Bread was baked fresh each day on an oven or hearth in the house or in the courtyard.

Below: An artist's cutaway illustration of a typical peasant house of Bible times.

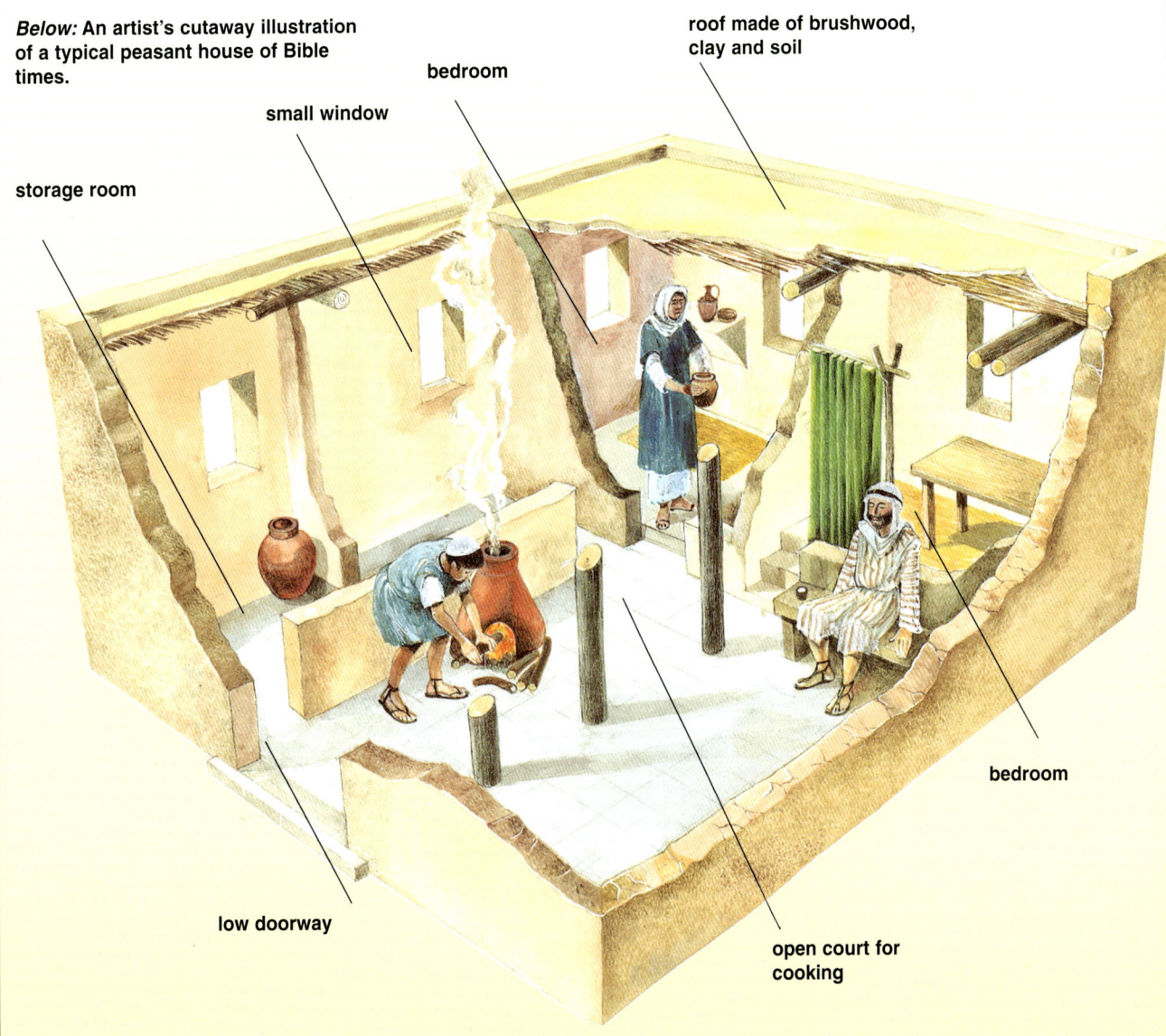

- storage room
- small window
- bedroom
- roof made of brushwood, clay and soil
- low doorway
- open court for cooking
- bedroom

Palestine IN JESUS' TIME

Herod the Great, who was trusted by the Romans, was king at the time of Jesus' birth. However, when he died in 4 BC, his cruel son Archelaus succeeded him in Judea, but was soon removed by the Romans. Herod's son, Herod Antipas, ruled Galilee and Perea; it was he who had John the Baptist executed (Mark 6:14-29). A third son of Herod, Philip, ruled Iturea and Trachonitis from Caesarea Philippi.

After the exile of Archelaus, Rome ruled Judea directly through officials called procurators, who lived at Caesarea, and only came to Jerusalem for special festivals. The Procurator Pontius Pilate was temporarily in Jerusalem when he sentenced Jesus to death (Luke 22:66–23:25).

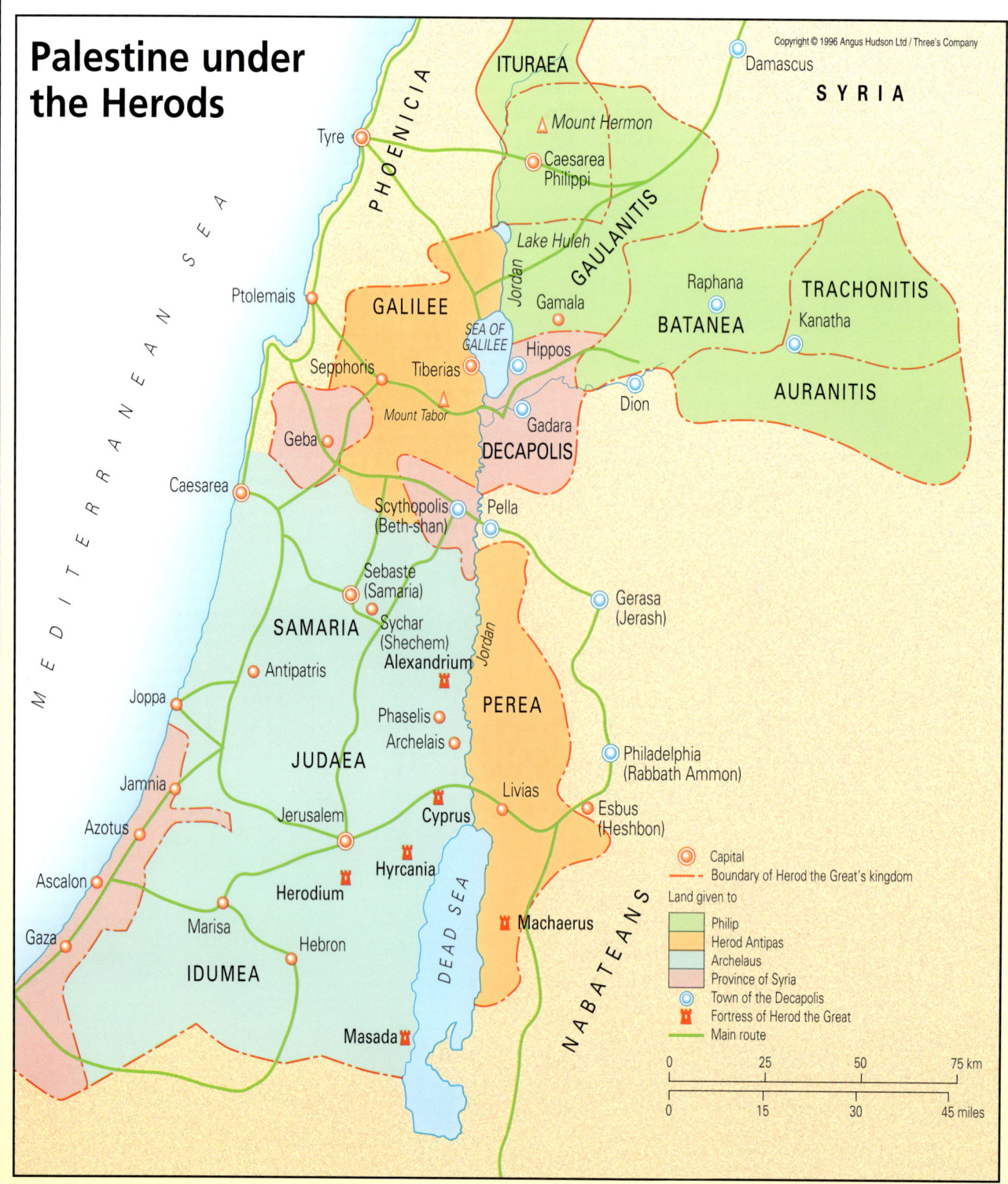

Jesus in Galilee

Jesus spent much of his ministry preaching and healing in Galilee. Although this Roman province was largely Jewish, many non-Jews also settled there. The Galileans, with a dialect of their own, were despised by many Jews from Jerusalem.

• In Jesus' time, many towns clustered around the **Sea of Galilee**. It was while sailing across the lake that Jesus calmed a sudden storm (Mark 4:35-41).

• Jesus came to live in **Capernaum** (Matthew 4:13), and cured a Roman officer's slave (Matthew 8:5-13), a leper (Matthew 8:2-4), Peter's mother-in-law (Matthew 8:14-15), a man with an evil spirit (Mark 1:21-26) and a paralysed man (Mark 2:1-12). Jesus preached in the Capernaum synagogue (Mark 1:21), called Matthew (Matthew 9:9) and paid the Temple tax here (Matthew 17:24), and denounced the town for its lack of faith (Matthew 11:23).

• In **Chorazin**, Jesus performed miracles, and later denounced the people for their lack of faith (Matthew 11:21)

• Jesus also visited **Bethsaida**, where he restored the sight of a blind man (Mark 8:22), and withdrew for a time of rest (Luke 9:10).

• At **Magdala**, Jesus was dining with Simon the Pharisee, when Mary anointed him (Luke 7:36-8:2).

• **Tabgha** may be the place where the risen Christ met the disciples and ate with them (John 21:1-14).

• The **Mount of Beatitudes** is the hill where, by tradition, Jesus taught the Sermon on the Mount (Matthew 5:1–7:29).

Jesus gathers his apostles and does many miracles here.

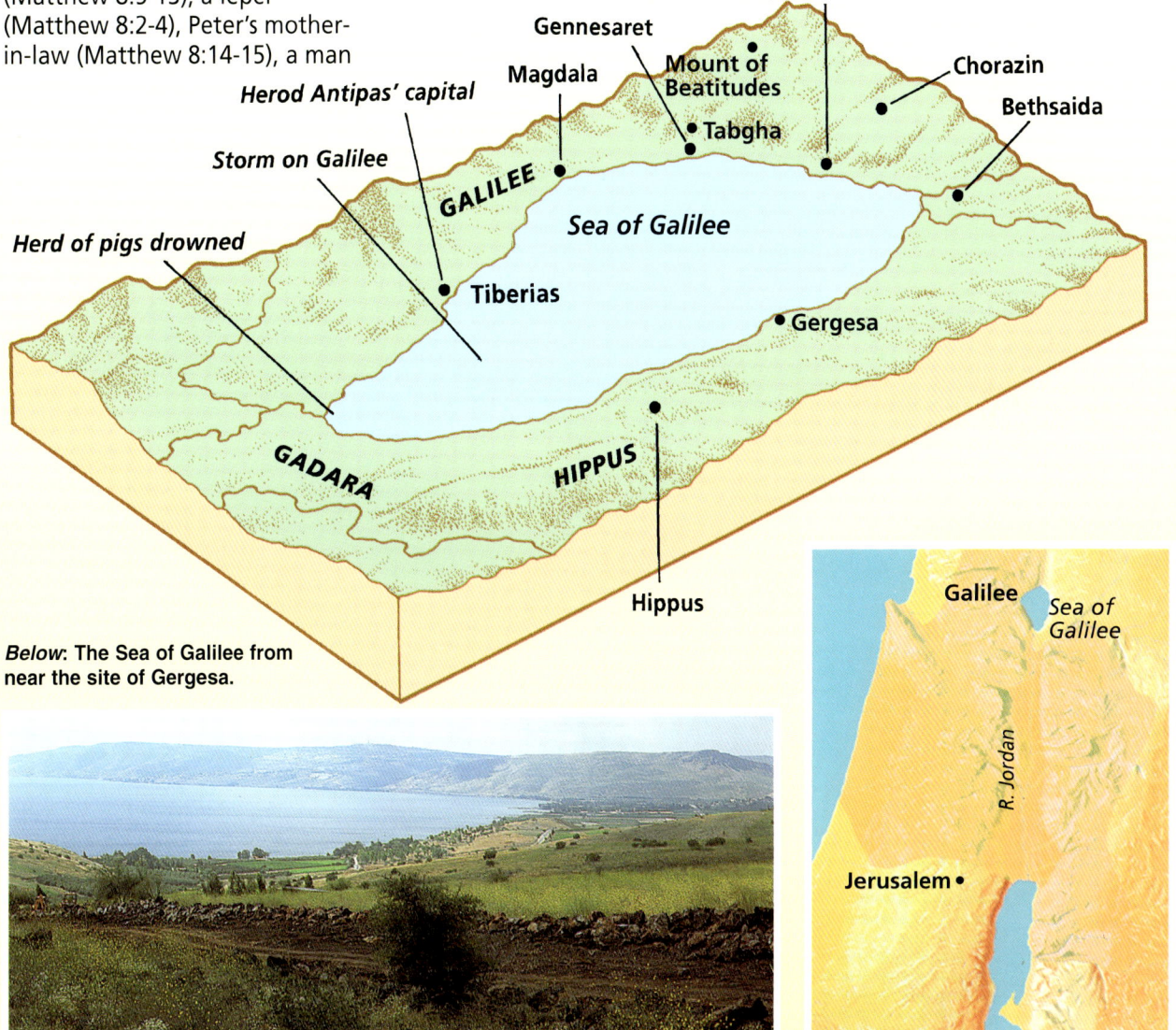

Below: **The Sea of Galilee from near the site of Gergesa.**

Parables of Jesus
EASY FINDER

What is a parable?
Parables make up about 35 per cent of Jesus' recorded sayings, so it is important to understand them. Jesus repeatedly uses illustrations from daily life in his parables, but the parables are not merely illustrations in his preaching; they are the preaching. Though the illustrations are drawn from familiar objects and events, they often include exaggeration and unexpected behaviour.

The Kingdom
The parables focus on God and his kingdom, and in doing so reveal what kind of God he is, the way in which he works and what he expects of human beings. Because many of the parables focus on the kingdom, some also reveal aspects of Jesus' mission. The parables are also intended to challenge and call to a decision; they are told in order to bring the listener to concede a point which he or she has not regarded as relevant to himself or herself.

Yet we also read in Mark 4:10-12 that Jesus taught in parables to conceal his message. Some are far from self-evident, and teaching in this way helped conceal Jesus' message from those hostile to him. Teaching by parable also offered an aid to the memory, and could serve to by-pass resistance in Jesus' listeners.

The following are Jesus' parables about the Kingdom.

Parables of the Kingdom	Matthew	Mark	Luke
The sower	13:3-9, 18-23	4:3-9, 13-20	8:5-8, 11-15
Growing seed		4:26-29	
Weeds	13:24-30, 36-43		
Mustard seed	13:31,32	4:30-32	13:18,19
Yeast	13:33		13:20,21
The pearl	13:45,46		
The hidden treasure	13:44		
The fishing net	13:47-50		
The unwilling children	11:16-19		7:31-35
The unfruitful fig tree			13:6-9
The workers in the vineyard	20:1-16		
The two brothers	21:28-32		
The royal wedding feast	22:1-14		
The great dinner			14:16-24
The wicked workers	21:33-46	12:1-12	20:9-19
Lost sheep	18:12-14		15:3-7
Lost coin			15:8-10
Lost son			15:11-32
The two creditors			7:41-47
The Pharisee and the tax-collector			18:9-14
The rich man and Lazarus			16:19-31
The watchful servants			12:35-40
Ten girls at a wedding	25:1-13		
The unreliable servant	24:45-51		12:42-46
The five talents	25:14-30		
The ten gold coins			19:11-27
The rich fool			12:16-21
Good Samaritan			10:25-37
The unforgiving servant	18:23-35		
The troublesome friend			11:5-8
The dishonest manager			16:1-13
The unjust judge			18:1-8

Miracles of Jesus
EASY FINDER

Three things are needed to make a true miracle: the event must be visible, the event must go beyond the powers of nature and the event must be the sign of a divine message.

Jesus did many miracles or signs. They show his power, his love for people and his desire to help. Jesus' miracles explained his mission, revealed his divinity, proved him to be the Messiah and began the world's renewal.

Miracles in John
John's Gospel records seven miracles, apart from the death and resurrection of Jesus. John chose particular miracles to help his readers see Jesus as the Son of God and to show the need to trust in him.

Healings	Matthew	Mark	Luke	John
Son of government official				4:46-54
Sick man at a pool				5:1-18
Man in synagogue		1:21-28	4:31-37	
Man with skin disease	8:1-4	1:40-45	5:12-14	
Roman officer's servant	8:5-13		7:1-10	
Dead son of a widow			7:11-15	
Peter's mother-in-law	8:14,15	1:29-31	4:38,39	
An uncontrollable man		5:1-20	8:26-39	
Paralysed man	9:1-8	2:1-12	5:17-26	
Woman with severe bleeding	9:20-22	5:25-34	8:43-48	
Dead girl	9:18-26	5:21-43	8:40-56	
Dumb man	9:32-34			
Man with a paralysed hand	12:9-14	3:1-6	6:6-11	
Blind and dumb man	12:22,23		11:14	
Canaanite woman's daughter	15:21-28	7:24-30		
Deaf and dumb man		7:31-37		
Blind man at Bethsaida		8:22-26		
Boy with epilepsy	17:14-20	9:14-29	9:37-43	
Blind Bartimaeus		10:46-52	18:35-43	
Woman with a bad back			13:10-17	
Sick man			14:1-6	
Man born blind				9:1-41
Dead friend named Lazarus				11:1-44
Slave's ear			22:49-51	
Crowd in Capernaum	8:16,17	1:32-34	4:40,41	
Two blind men	9:27-31			
Crowd by Lake Galilee		3:7-12		
Crowd on the hillsides by Galilee	15:29-31			
Ten men			17:11-19	
Control over laws of nature				
Water changed into wine				2:1-11
Catch of fish			5:1-11	
Jesus calms a storm	8:23-27	4:35-41	8:22-25	
5,000 men alone are fed	14:13-21	6:30-44	9:10-17	6:1-15
Jesus walks on the water	14:22-33	6:45-52		6:16-21
4,000 men alone are fed	15:32-39	8:1-10		
A fish and the payment of taxes	17:24-27			
Fig tree withers away	21:18-22	11:12-14, 20-24		
Another catch of fish				21:1-11
Christ conquers death	28:1-10	16:1-11	24:1-12	20:1-18

The Synagogue

In Jesus' time, there was at least one synagogue in nearly every town and village (Luke 4:14-30). The Jews started having services in synagogues during the Exile, when they had no access to the Temple. The synagogues developed their own form of service, parallel to that of the Temple.

There were synagogue services every Sabbath, and on the Jewish festival days. The synagogue was also open for prayer three times a day.

In the main room of the synagogue stood a seven-branched lampstand, or *Menorah*, and a lamp of eternity. During worship there would be prayers, Scripture readings and praise.

The sacred rolls of the Law (the *Torah*) were kept in a special cupboard.

Sometimes in larger buildings there would be a courtyard with small rooms leading off it built onto the main structure.

Women and children
Women and children were allowed only into the gallery of the synagogue.

Above: The fourth-century Capernaum synagogue has been carefully excavated and partially reconstructed.

Below: An artist's cutaway illustration of a synagogue from around the time of Jesus.

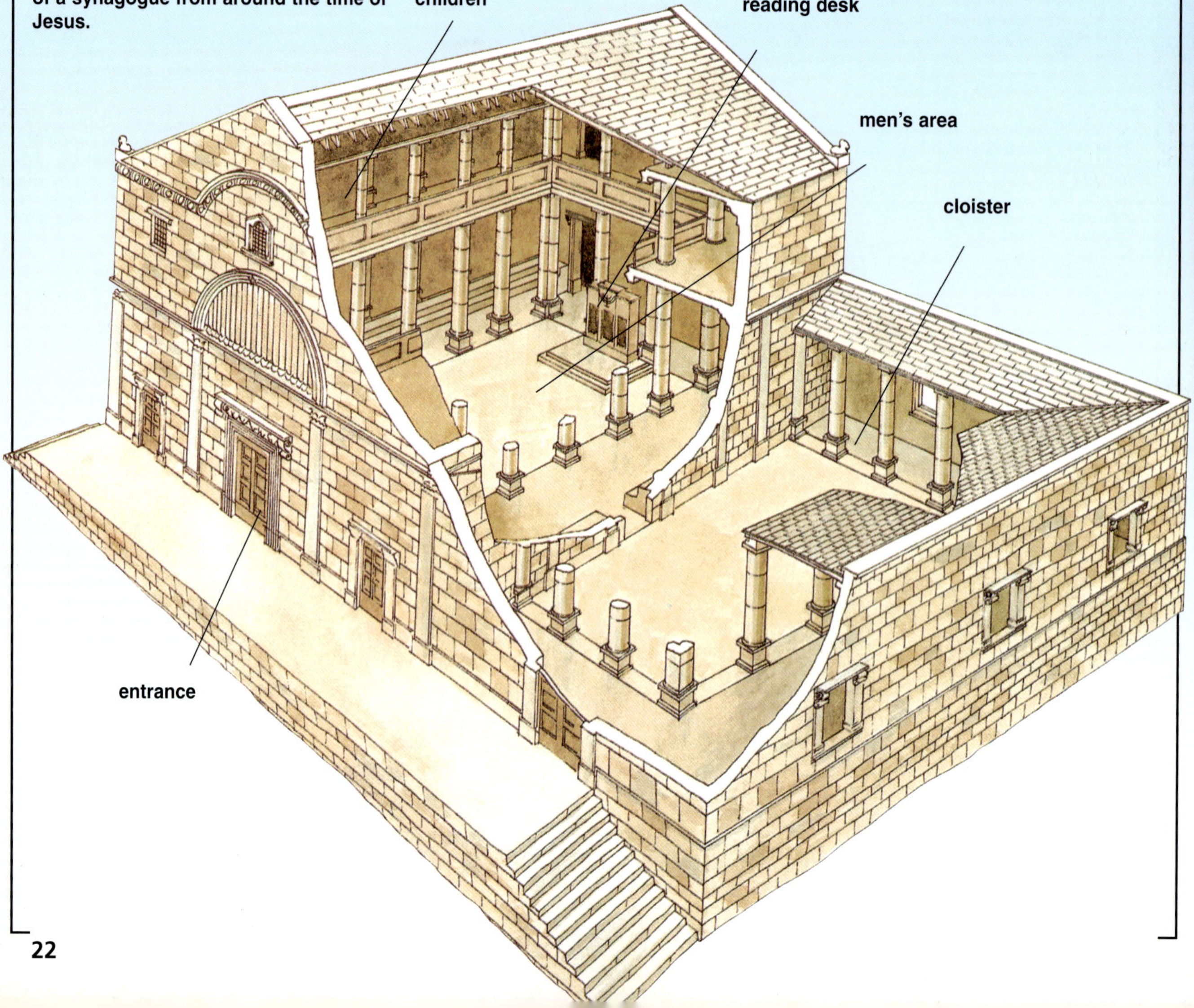

- gallery for women and children
- reading desk
- men's area
- cloister
- entrance

Herod's Temple

Around 20 BC, Herod the Great embarked on reconstructing the Temple in Jerusalem. First, the Temple Mount area on which the Temple stood was doubled in size in a huge earth-moving operation.

The new Temple was magnificent, constructed in white marble and decorated in gold. Its plan was similar to Solomon's Temple, with the Holy Place and the Holiest Place within, the latter only visited once a year, only by the high priest.

Although anyone could enter the outer Court of the Gentiles, only Jewish people were allowed inside the inner courtyards. The Court of the Gentiles was a market-place, where visitors bought and sold, and changed their money into special coins needed for offerings and for the temple tax (Mark 11:15-17).

Below: **Photograph of a magnificent accurate scale model of Herod's Temple, built by a farmer in England.**

By permission A. Garrard

Jerusalem
JESUS' LAST DAYS

Saturday: Supper at Bethany.

Sunday: The triumphal entry into Jerusalem, seated on a donkey (Mark 11).

Monday: Jesus cleanses the Temple of the money-changers and merchants (Mark 11).

Tuesday: Jesus teaches in the Temple (John 12). Judas agrees with the high priests that he will betray Jesus.

Wednesday: Quiet day in Bethany.

Thursday: The Last Supper with the twelve apostles in an upper room in Jerusalem. After the meal, Jesus takes them to the Garden of Gethsemane, across the Kidron Valley, to pray. He is arrested after Judas betrays him with a kiss (Matthew 26).

Friday: Jesus is tried before the high priests (Matthew 26), and is then taken to the Sanhedrin, the Court of the Jews. Next, he is taken for trial before Pontius Pilate (Luke 23), who sends him to Herod for a hearing. Finally, after Pilate has sentenced Jesus to death, he is taken to Golgotha, the place of crucifixion (Mark 15).

After his body has been taken down from the cross, Jesus is buried in the tomb of the rich Jew, Joseph of Arimathea (Luke 23).

Sunday: Disciples see the risen Christ in Jerusalem (Luke 24).

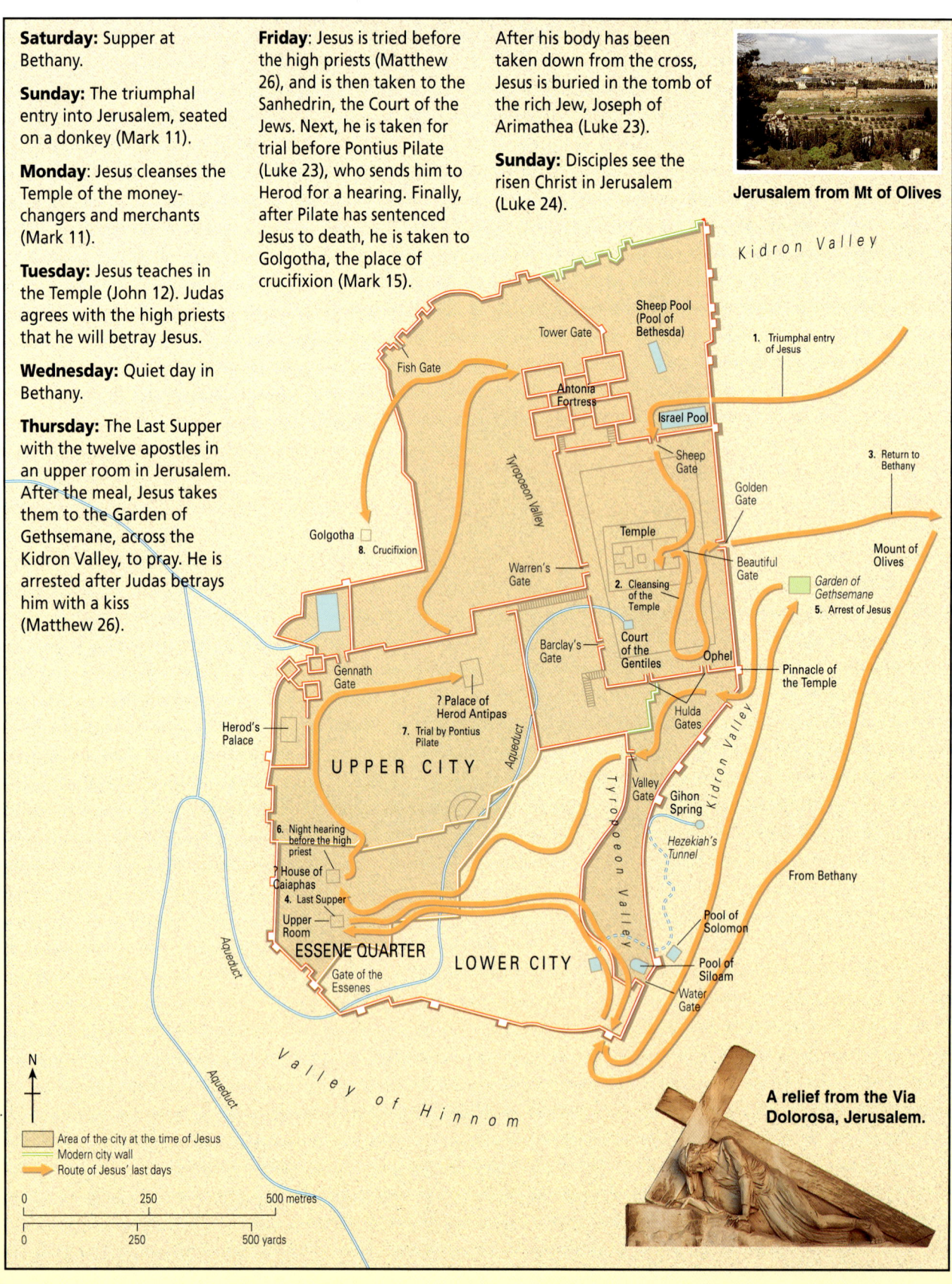

Jerusalem from Mt of Olives

A relief from the Via Dolorosa, Jerusalem.

Jesus' Resurrection APPEARANCES

The Gospels do not describe the resurrection itself; but they recount the meetings of many different people with the risen Christ. Many reliable witnesses claimed to have seen Jesus alive after his death (1 Corinthians 15:3-8).

Mary Magdalene.

Mary.

The Garden Tomb, Jerusalem, is probably similar to the tomb in which Jesus was buried.

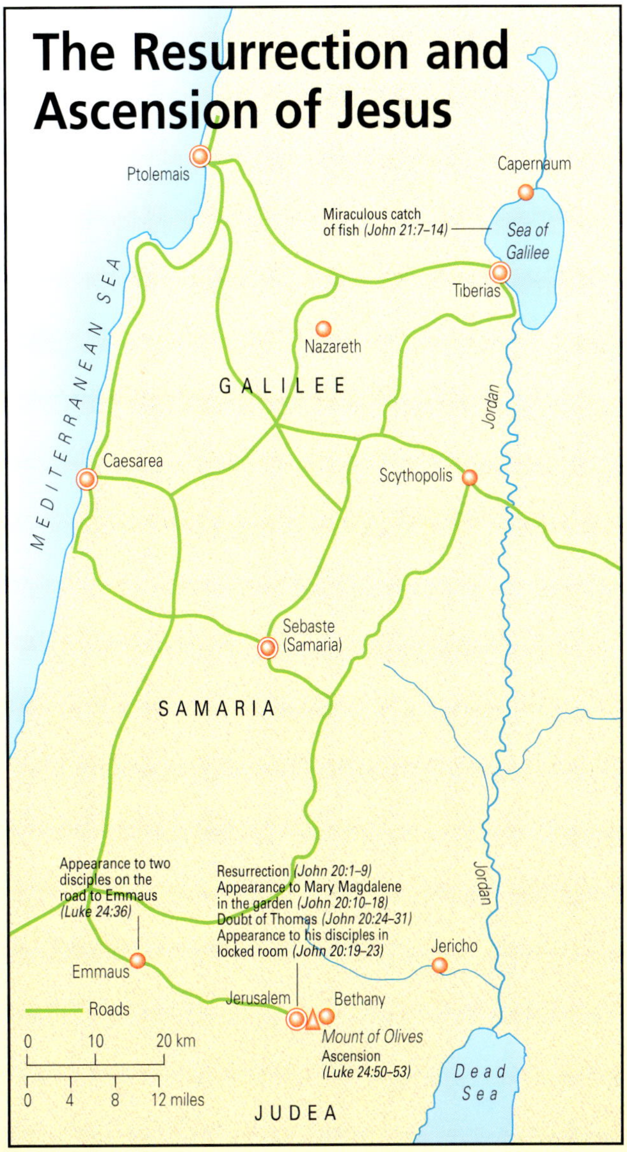

The following people all met the risen Christ:

1. Mary Magdalene (John 20:11-18).

2. Simon Peter (Luke 24:34).

3. Simon Peter (Luke 24:34).

4. The disciples – apart from Thomas (John 20:19-23).

5. The disciples – including Thomas (John 20:24-29).

6. Mary Magdalene and 'the other Mary' (Matthew 28:1-10).

7. The apostles in Galilee (Matthew 28:16-17).

8. Seven disciples by the Sea of Tiberias (John 21:1-14).

9. More than five hundred of his followers (1 Corinthians 15:6).

10. James (1 Corinthians 15:7).

11. His disciples (Acts 1:4-9).

12. Paul (Acts 9:1-9).

The Resurrection and Ascension of Jesus

The roof of the Church of the Holy Sepulchre, Jerusalem.

PAUL'S MISSIONARY JOURNEYS

Paul's First Journey
Paul travelled with Barnabas. They went first to Cyprus, Barnabas' home, and then to Asia Minor, preaching wherever they went, and leaving communities of believers behind (Acts 13:1–14:28).

Top: Paul was mistaken for Hermes (Mercury) the messenger of the gods when he preached at Lystra.

Paul's Second Journey
Paul took with him the young man Timothy. He returned to many places he had visited before, but crossed into Greece, bringing the gospel to Europe for the first time, visiting the great cities of Corinth and Athens (Acts 15:36–18:22).

Bottom: The Acropolis, Athens, viewed from the Areopagus, where the apostle Paul preached.

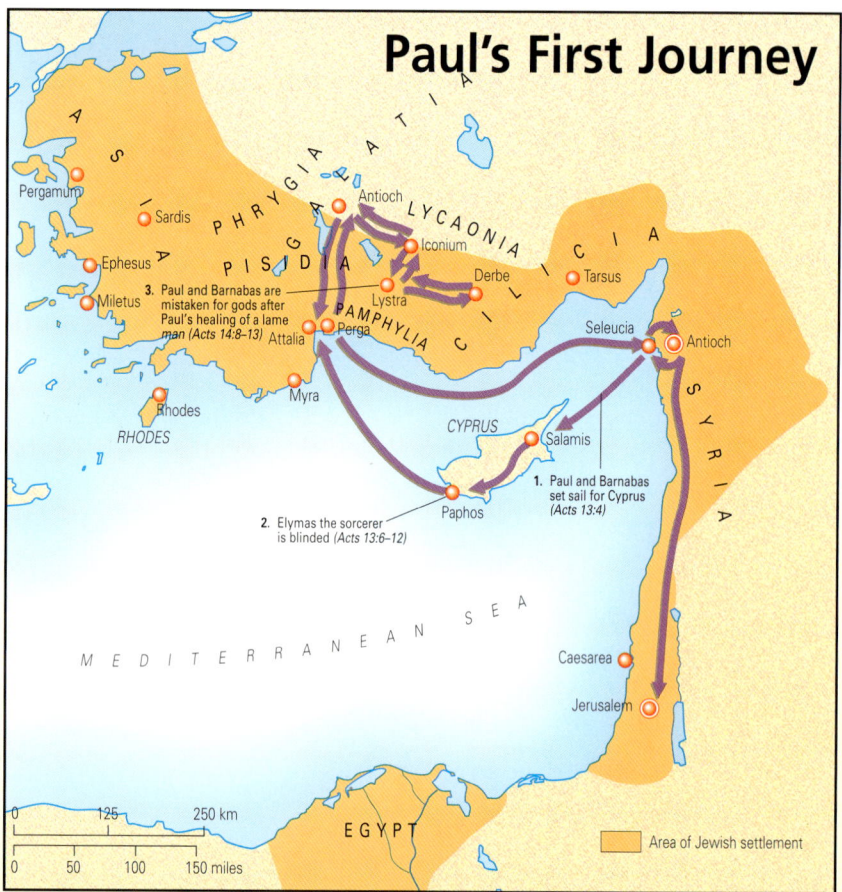

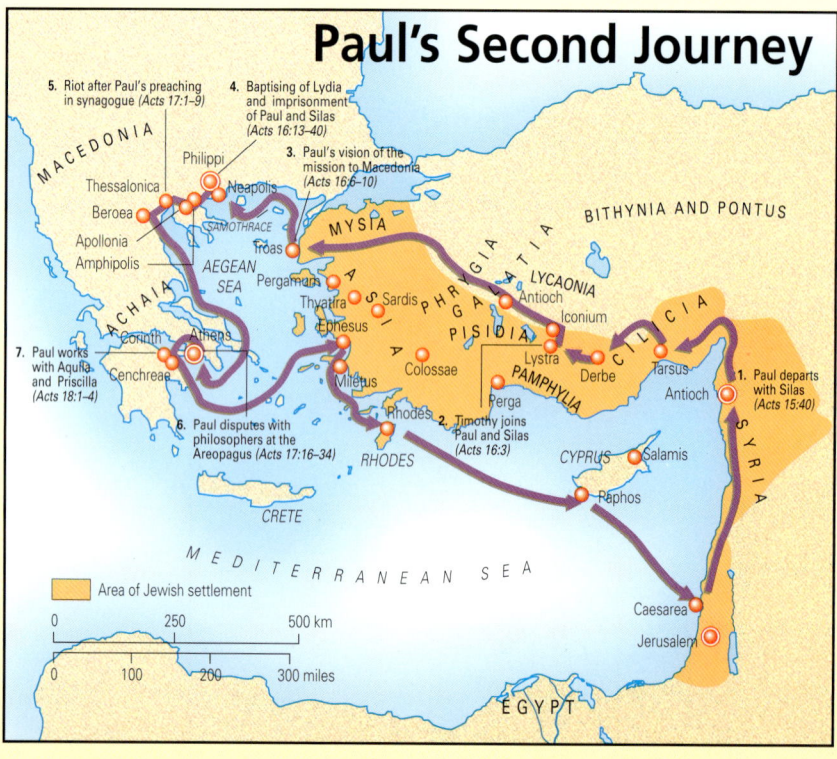

Paul's Third Journey

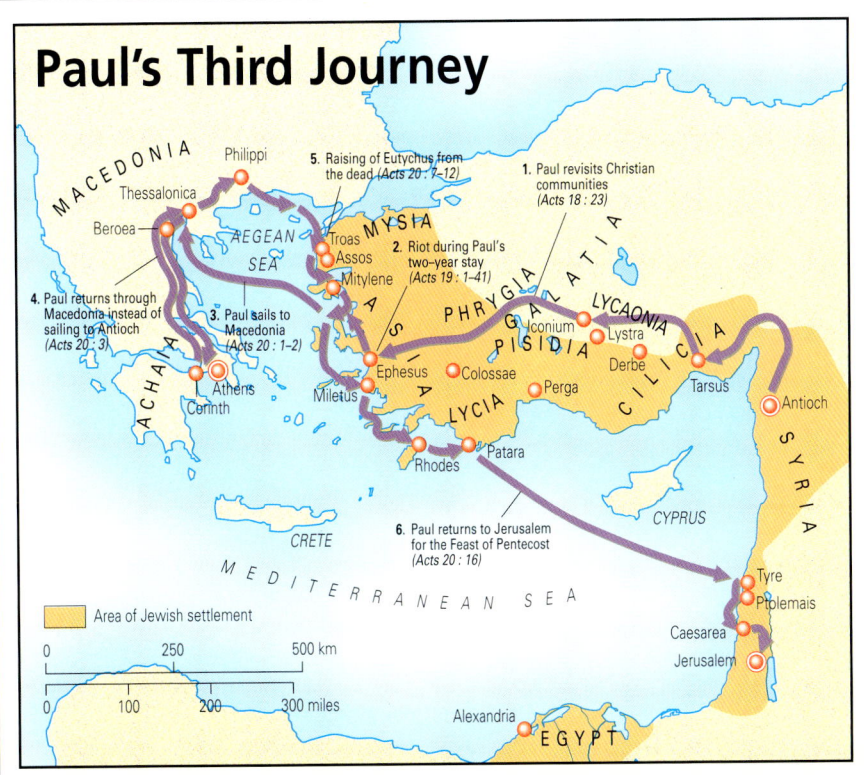

Map labels:
1. Paul revisits Christian communities (Acts 18:23)
2. Riot during Paul's two-year stay (Acts 19:1-41)
3. Paul sails to Macedonia (Acts 20:1-2)
4. Paul returns through Macedonia instead of sailing to Antioch (Acts 20:3)
5. Raising of Eutychus from the dead (Acts 20:7-12)
6. Paul returns to Jerusalem for the Feast of Pentecost (Acts 20:16)

Paul's Third Journey

Paul stayed in the city of Ephesus for two years, working and teaching the faith. He also returned to places he had visited previously. When he returned to Jerusalem, he was arrested and imprisoned for two years (Acts 18:23–21:16).

Paul's voyage to Rome

In an attempt to gain his release, Paul appealed to Caesar, and was sent to Rome. After an eventful voyage, during which he was shipwrecked, he finally reached Rome, where it is believed he was eventually executed (Acts 27:1–28:31).

Below inset: The ancient Forum, Rome, centre of the mighty Roman Empire.

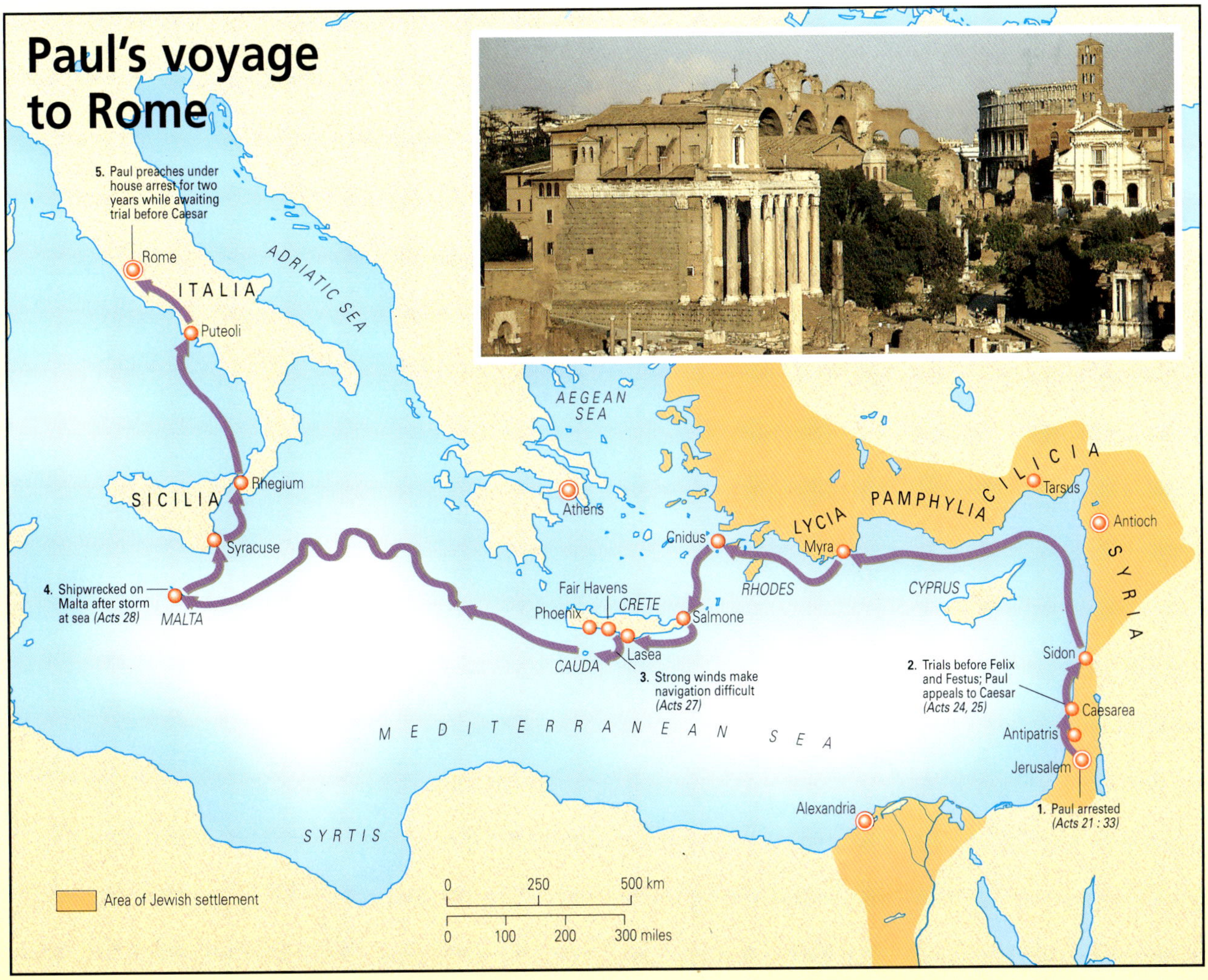

Paul's voyage to Rome

Map labels:
1. Paul arrested (Acts 21:33)
2. Trials before Felix and Festus; Paul appeals to Caesar (Acts 24, 25)
3. Strong winds make navigation difficult (Acts 27)
4. Shipwrecked on Malta after storm at sea (Acts 28)
5. Paul preaches under house arrest for two years while awaiting trial before Caesar

The Good News Travels

After the coming of the Holy Spirit on the day of Pentecost, the believers in Jerusalem began to preach boldly and increased in numbers daily (Acts 2:1-47). The Jewish leaders tried to stop them, but in fact helped the young movement to spread (Acts 4:1-31).

Stephen, a leader of the church in Jerusalem, was accused of blasphemy and the Jews had him stoned to death (Acts 6:1–8:2). Believers in Jerusalem were persecuted, and many fled – south into Judea, north to Samaria, and west to the coast and even as far as Cyprus (Acts 8:1-3, 11:19). Many of the apostles also left Jerusalem and preached elsewhere. Philip, Peter and John all made conversions in Samaria (Acts 8), a 'no-go' area for religious (or 'strict') Jews.

Philip set out for Gaza, baptizing an official from Ethiopia, before moving on to preach in the coastal towns (Acts 8:26-40).

Peter travelled to Caesarea, where he was shown in a vision that he should take the gospel to the Gentiles (Acts 10:1-48). As the persecution of Christians by Jews in Jerusalem became more evident so Jewish Christians dispersed northwards. They had reached as far as Antioch, third largest city in the Roman Empire, by the time Paul embarked on his missionary journeys (Acts 13).

Paul's Journey to Damascus

Some time after Stephen's death, while Paul (then Saul) was still a Pharisee, he got permission from the Temple authorities to go to Damascus to search out Christians (Acts 9:1-2). It was on the way there that he received his blinding vision of the risen Christ. After regaining his sight in Damascus with the help of Ananias in Straight Street, Paul became a Christian and was himself forced to flee for his life back to Jerusalem (Acts 9:23-26). He was soon in danger again, from Hellenist Jews, and departed for his home town of Tarsus via Caesarea.

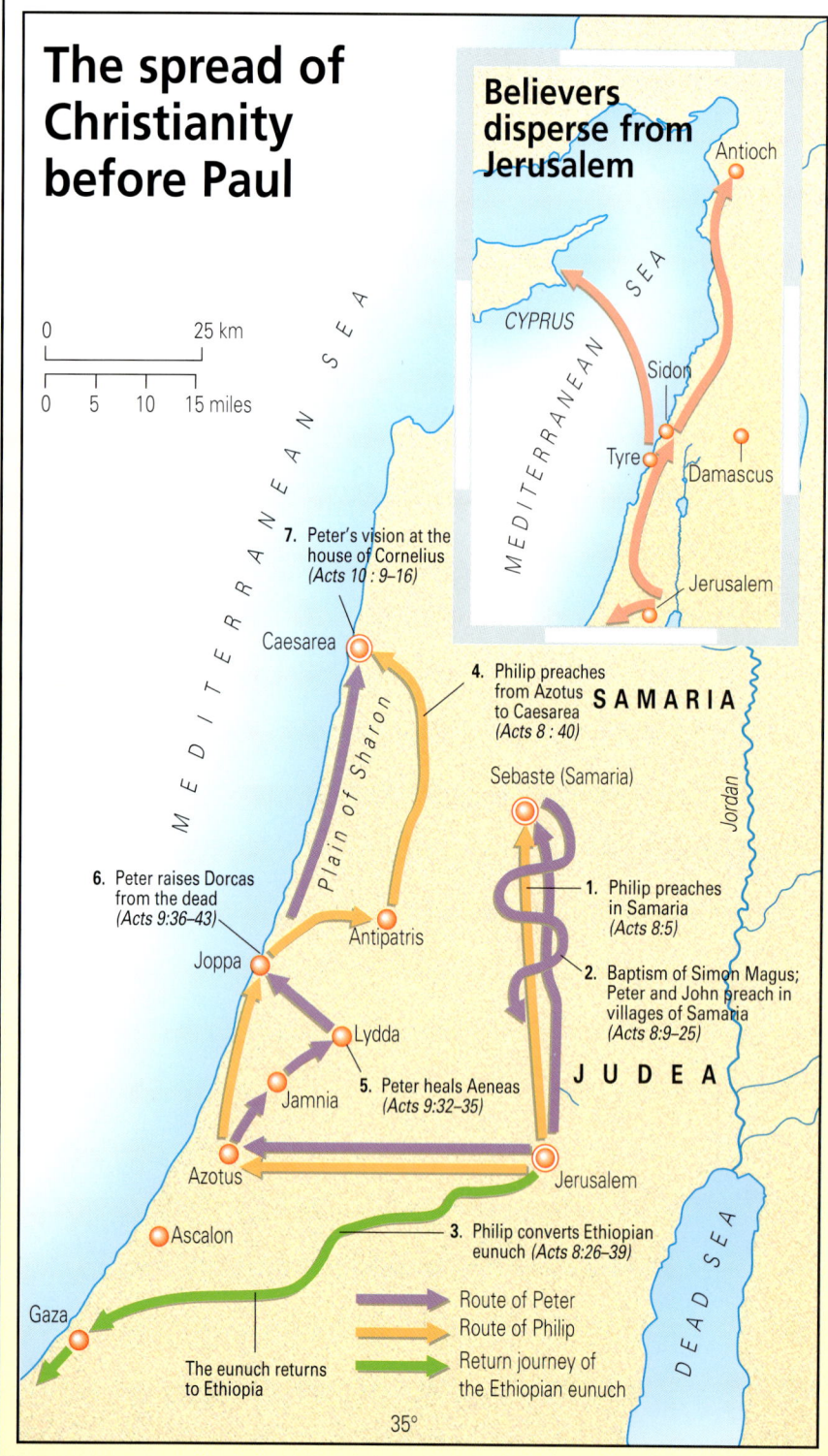

Travel in Bible Times

In Jesus' time, most people travelled on foot. Those who could afford it travelled on horseback or in horse-drawn carriages. Palestine is a bare, hilly country, which is difficult for travel. Walkers could usually cover 16-20 Roman miles (15-18 miles/24-30 km) per day. Jesus travelled on foot around Galilee, and Paul walked long distances taking the gospel to new places.

Sometimes travellers were carried in chairs hung on poles and supported on slaves' shoulders. The rich also travelled in horse-drawn carriages, and merchants used heavy carts to transport grain and other goods. Asses and mules were also useful for carrying loads.

By Jesus' time, the Romans were building large sailing vessels. When Paul was taken to Rome (Acts 27:1-44), he travelled in a grain-ship which carried 276 people. Such vessels had a single main sail, and were difficult to handle in bad weather.

Below: **A passenger carriage from Roman times.**

Above: **Wealthy people could be carried in a litter, supported on slaves' shoulders.**

Above: **A goods cart drawn by two oxen.**

People of the NEW TESTAMENT

Andrew
Peter's fisherman brother, and one of the twelve apostles.
Matthew 4:18, 10:2; John 1:35-44, 6:8-9, 12:20-22; Acts 1:12-14

Aquila
A tent-maker and Jewish Christian friend of Paul; husband of Priscilla.
Acts 18:1-3, 18-26

Barnabas
Barnabas was a nickname for Joses, a Jewish Christian who was born in Cyprus, and who travelled extensively with Paul on his missionary work. His name means 'son of encouragement'.
Acts 4:36-37, 9:27, 11:22-30, 13:1–15:39; 1 Corinthians 9:6; Galatians 2:1-13

Caiaphas
The high priest in Jerusalem who found Jesus guilty of blasphemy and sent him to Pilate for sentence.
Matthew 26:3-5, 57-68; John 11:49-53

Cleopas
One of the disciples who met the risen Christ on the Emmaus road.
Luke 24:13-35

Cornelius
A Roman centurion, stationed at Caesarea, who was converted to Christianity.
Acts 10:1-48

Dorcas
A disciple in Joppa who did much good among the poor and widows. When she died, Peter came and restored her to life.
Acts 9:36-42

Elizabeth
Wife of the priest Zechariah, and mother, in old age, of John the Baptist.
Luke 1:5-66

Herod the Great
Herod was king of Judea at the time of Jesus' birth. Trusted by the Romans, he undertook a huge building programme in Judea. He ordered the killing of male children to eliminate any rival.
Matthew 2:1-20; Luke 1:5

Herod the Tetrarch
Son of Herod the Great, he imprisoned, and later beheaded, John the Baptist. Pilate sent Jesus to him for trial, since Jesus came from Galilee, Herod's territory.
Matthew 14:1-12; Luke 9:7-9, 13:31-32, 23:6-15

James
Jesus' brother. After Pentecost, he became a leader of the Jerusalem church, and he may be the writer of the letter of James.
Matthew 13:55; Acts 15:13-21; James

James
James was a fisherman, like his brother John. Called by Jesus to follow him as one of the twelve apostles, he was present at Jesus' transfiguration. He was executed by Herod Agrippa.
Matthew 4:21-22; Mark 1:19-20; Luke 9:28-36; Acts 12:1-3

James
Son of Alphaeus and one of the twelve apostles.
Matthew 10:3

John
James' brother, and another fisherman, John was 'the disciple whom Jesus loved'. Jesus told him to look after Mary, his mother, when he was dying on the cross. John is believed to be the writer of John's Gospel, 1, 2 and 3 John and Revelation.
Matthew 4:21-22, 10:2, 17:1-13; Mark 10:35-45; Luke 22:8; John; Acts 3:1-10, 4:1-31; 1,2,3 John, Revelation

John the Baptist
John was sent to prepare the way for Jesus, the Messiah. He lived simply, and preached repentance and baptism. He was imprisoned and beheaded by Herod the Tetrarch.
Matthew 3:1-15, 11:2-19, 14:1-12; Luke 1:5-17, 3:1-20, 7:18-35

Judas Iscariot
Judas was one of the twelve apostles. His second name means 'man from Kerioth', a town close to Hebron. Judas betrayed Jesus, and later hanged himself.
Matthew 10:2-4, 26:47-49, 27:1-10; John 12:4-7, 13:26-30

Lazarus
The brother of Mary and Martha, Lazarus lived in Bethany and was raised from the dead by Jesus.
John 11:1-44

Lydia
A business woman from Thyatira who traded in costly purple cloth, Lydia was converted through the preaching of Paul
Acts 16:12-15,40

Martha
The sister of Mary and Lazarus, Martha lived with her siblings in Bethany.
Luke 10:38-42; John 11:1-44

Mary
Mother of Jesus and wife of Joseph. Her song of faith, called the *Magnificat*, is found in Luke 1. When he was dying on the cross, Jesus told John to care for his mother.
Matthew 1:16-25; Luke 1:26-56, 2:1-39; John 2:1-5, 19:25-27; Acts 1:14

Mary
The sister of Martha, Mary anointed Jesus with oil just before his death.
Luke 10:38-42; John 11:1-44, 12:1-8

Mary Magdalene
From Magdala in Galilee, Mary was healed by Jesus. Later, she was the first to meet the risen Christ.
Matthew 27:56,61, 28:1-10; Luke 8:1-3; John 20:1-18

Matthew
Matthew, or Levi, was a tax-collector who was called by Jesus to become one of the twelve apostles. He is believed to be the author of the first Gospel.
Matthew 9:9-13, 10:3; Mark 2:13-17; Luke 5:27-32

Nicodemus
A Pharisee and ruler of the Jews, Nicodemus came to talk to Jesus secretly by night, and later assisted at his burial.
John 3:1-36, 7:50-52, 19:38-42

Paul
Paul was born in Tarsus, and brought up as a strict Pharisee. Suddenly converted to Christ on the road to Damascus, he became the great missionary to the Gentiles. He undertook three major missionary journeys, founding and building up Christian communities wherever he went. He wrote letters to many new churches to encourage them in the faith. Paul was executed by Nero in Rome about AD 67.
Acts 7:1–28:31; Romans–Philemon

Peter (Simon Peter)
Peter was a fisherman called by Jesus to become one of the twelve apostles. After the resurrection, Christ appeared specially to Peter, who became a leader of the young church. He wrote 1 and 2 Peter, and was probably executed in Rome.
Matthew 4:18-2, 16:13–17:8, 26:31-35, 69-75; John 13:1-9,24,31-38, 21:1-22; Acts 1:13–5:42, 8:14-25, 9:32–12:18, 15:1-11; 1 and 2 Peter

Philip
One of the twelve apostles, Philip came from Bethsaida in Galilee.
Matthew 10:3; John 1:43-46, 6:7, 12:20-22

Pontius Pilate
Pilate was the Roman procurator of Judea who sentenced Jesus to death, though he declared him to be innocent.
Matthew 27:11-26; John 18:28-36

Priscilla
Wife of Aquila; a faithful Jewish Christian and friend of Paul.
Acts 18:1-3, 18-26

Silas
Silas was a leader of the Jerusalem church, and went with Paul on his second missionary journey.
Acts 15:22–18:22

Stephen
A Greek-speaking Jew and one of the seven men chosen to help the apostles in Jerusalem, Stephen became the first martyr in the church. *Acts 6:1-8:2*

Tabitha
Also known as **Dorcas** (see entry).

Thomas
Thomas was one of the twelve apostles, and was initially very sceptical when the risen Christ appeared after the crucifixion.
Matthew 10:3; Mark 3:18; John 11:16, 20:24-29, 21:2

Timothy
Timothy was a young convert of Paul, who accompanied the apostle on his second missionary journey. He later led the church in Ephesus. Paul wrote 1 and 2 Timothy to him.
Acts 16:1–18:22; 1 and 2 Timothy

Titus
A Gentile convert, sent as a missionary to Crete. Paul wrote a letter to him.
2 Corinthians 2:13; Galatians 2:1-3; Titus

Zacchaeus
A wealthy and dishonest tax-collector, Zacchaeus climbed a tree in Jericho to see Jesus. When Jesus invited himself to his home, Zacchaeus made full restitution.
Luke 19:1-10

THE SEVEN CHURCHES OF Asia Minor

The first three chapters of Revelation consist of letters to seven churches in Asia Minor.

Ephesus
With a population of up to 500,000, Ephesus was the leading port of Asia Minor, famed for the worship of Artemis, whose priestesses were cult prostitutes (Revelation 2:1-7).

Smyrna
This ancient port (modern Izmir) had a population of c. 200,000, and a wealthy academic community. Smyrna boasted a 'street of gold' with a temple at each end (2:8-11).

Pergamum
With the second largest library in the Roman Empire, Pergamum was famous for parchment, and as the site of the Asclepion (health resort), and altar of Zeus (2:12-17).

Thyatira
A city of many trade guilds, located on an imperial post road (2:18-29).

Sardis
A wealthy fortress city set on a hill, accessible to a fertile river basin, Thyatira was rebuilt by Tiberius (3:1-6).

Philadelphia
A fortress city on an imperial post road, Philadelphia was an educational centre for Hellenism (3:7-13).

Laodicea
The producer of world-famous black wool, Laodicea was a banking centre which also had a medical school (3:14-22).

The Library of Celsus, Ephesus.

The Gymnasium, Sardis.

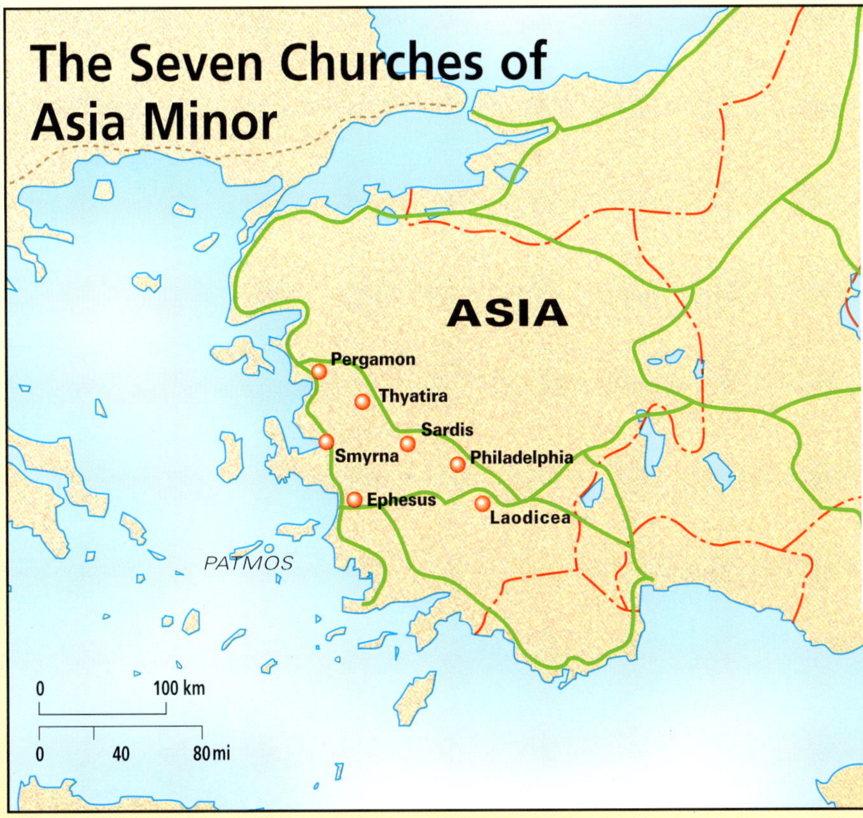

Top: Little remains of Laodicea.
Bottom: Forum, ancient Izmir.

Index

Aaron 15
Abram, see Abraham
Abraham 4, 5, 15
Adam 15
Andrew 30
Animals 12
Apocrypha 2
Aquila 30
Aramaic 3
Ark of the Covenant 10, 11
Assyria 4, 14
Atonement, Day of 13

Babylon 4
Barnabas 30
Beatitudes, Mount of 19
Bethsaida 19
Bible 2
Bible, writing the 3

Caiaphas 30
Capernaum 19, 22
Chorazin 19
Cleopas 30
Clothing 16
Cornelius 30
Court of the Gentiles 23

Daily life in Bible times 17
Damascus 26
Daniel 15
David 8, 15
Dead Sea Scrolls 3
Deborah 15
Deuterocanonical books 2
Divided Kingdom 9
Dorcas 30

Egypt 5, 6
Elijah 15
Elisha 15
Elizabeth 30
Ephesus 31
Esther 15
Eve 15
Exile, The 4

Exodus 6
Ezekiel 15
Ezra 15

Farming 12
Feasts, Jewish 13
Festivals, Jewish 13
Fruit 12

Galilee 19
Garden Tomb 25
Gideon 15
Grain 12
Greek 3

Harvest 12
Hebrew 3
Herod Antipas 18
Herod the Great 18, 23, 30
Herod the Tetrarch 30
Hezekiah 15
History, books of the Bible 2
Holiest Place 10, 11, 23
Holy Place 10, 11, 23
Holy Spirit 26
Houses 17
Housework 17

Incense, altar of 10, 11
Isaac 5, 15
Isaiah 15
Israel 4, 8, 9

Jacob 4, 5, 15
James 30
Jeremiah 15
Jerusalem 4, 8, 24
Jesus, birth of 18
Jesus, crucifixion of 24
Jesus, in Galilee 19
Jesus, last week of 24
Jesus, resurrection appearances of 25
John, the apostle 30
John, the Baptist 30
Jonah 15

Joseph 5, 15
Joshua 7, 15
Judah 4, 9
Judas Iscariot 30
Judges 4

Kingdom of God 20
Kings 4, 8, 9, 14
Koine Greek 3

Lampstands 10, 11
Laodicea 31
Last Supper 24
Lazarus 30
Law, books of the Bible 2
Letters, of Paul 2
Lydia 30

Magdala 19
Martha 30
Mary, Magdalene 25, 30
Mary, mother of Jesus 30
Mary, sister of Martha 30
Matthew 30
Miracles of Jesus 21
Miriam 15
Missionary journeys of Paul 28-29
Moses 4, 6, 15

New Testament 2
Nicodemus 30

Old Testament 2
Ostraca 3

Palestine 18
Parables of Jesus 20
Passover 13
Paul 25, 26, 28-29, 30
Pentecost 13, 26
Pergamum 31
Peter 25, 26, 30
Philip 26, 30
Philadelphia 31
Philistines 7
Poetry, books of the Bible 2

Pontius Pilate 30
Priscilla 30
Promised Land 5, 7
Prophecy 2
Prophets 8, 14
Purim 13

Qumran 3

Rebekah 15
Revelation, book of 2
Rome 29
Ruth 15

Samuel 15
Sarah 5, 15
Sardis 31
Saul 8
Showbread, table of 10, 11
Silas 30
Smyrna 31
Solomon 8, 11, 15
Stephen 26, 30
Synagogues 22

Tabernacle 10, 11
Tabitha 30
Temple, Herod's 23
Temple, Solomon's 8, 11
Ten Commandments 6, 10
Tent of God's presence 10
Thomas 25, 30
Thyatira 32
Time chart, Old Testament 8
Timothy 28, 30
Titus 30
Travel in Bible times 27

Wisdom, books of the Bible 2
Writing implements 3
Writing of the Bible 3

Zacchaeus 30

Copyright © 1999 Angus Hudson Ltd/ Tim Dowley & Peter Wyart trading as Three's Company

All rights reserved. No part of this publication may be reproduced, stored in a retrieval system, or transmitted in any form or by any means – for example, electronic, photocopy, recording – without the prior written permission of the publisher. The only exception is brief quotations in printed reviews.

Published in the UK by
Candle Books 1999
Distributed by STL
PO Box 300
Carlisle, Cumbria, CA3 0QS
ISBN 1-85985-333-1

Designed by Peter Wyart

Worldwide coedition organised and produced by
Angus Hudson Ltd,
Concorde House, Grenville Place,
Mill Hill, London NW7 3SA, England
Tel: +44 20 8959 3668
Fax +44 20 8959 3678

Printed in Singapore